Emma Heathcote-James is a theology graduate whose groundbreaking findings formed the basis to her bestselling debut *Seeing Angels*, which the *Daily Mail* hailed as 'an extraordinary, intelligent book'. She followed this up with the critically-acclaimed *After-Death Communication*, which further explored the spiritual dimension beyond physical death and her most recent book is *Psychic Pets*, a fascinating investigation into how animal intuition and perception has changed human lives. A regular contributor to national and international radio and television programmes, Emma has researched and presented her findings on the BBC's *Everyman* programme.

AN INVESTIGATION INTO THE
PHENOMENON OF AFTER-DEATH
MATERIALISATION

THEY
WALK
AMONG
US

EMMA HEATHCOTE-JAMES

metro

Published by Metro Publishing
An imprint of John Blake Publishing Ltd,
3 Bramber Court, 2 Bramber Road,
London W14 9PB, England

www.johnblakepublishing.co.uk

www.facebook.com/Johnblakepub facebook
Twitter @johnblakepub twitter

First published in hardback 2004
Paperback edition published 2011

ISBN: 978 1 84358 391 2

British Library Cataloguing-in-Publication Data:

A catalogue record for this book is available from the British Library.

Design by www.envydesign.co.uk

Printed and bound by CPI Group (UK) Ltd, Croydon, CR0 4YY

1 3 5 7 9 10 8 6 4 2

Papers used by John Blake Publishing are natural, recyclable products made from
wood grown in sustainable forests. The manufacturing processes conform to the
environmental regulations of the country of origin.

Every attempt has been made to contact the relevant copyright-holders, but some
were unobtainable. We would be grateful if the appropriate people could contact us.

Written for the three people whose dedication, work and support made this book possible – John Samson, Michael Roll and, of course, Ronald Pearson.

'What most people believe to be the other side I consider home...
we are all just working our way back.'

SAM DI PAOLO

FOR THOSE WHO UNDERSTAND,

NO EXPLANATION IS NECESSARY;

FOR THOSE WHO DON'T UNDERSTAND,

NO EXPLANATION WILL SUFFICE.

CONTENTS

They Walk Among Us

'With Emma Heathcote-James we embark upon the most important and exciting quest of all, to find out what kind of beings we are, and whether or not we have a future after death. It is a journey requiring courage and an open mind, taking the reader through research past and present, and on to a new vision of humanity and the universe.'

MARIANNE RANKIN, CHAIR, ALISTER HARDY SOCIETY

'I found this book to be pure gold – it is very interesting and most informative, highly educational and satisfies our desire to understand the greatest challenge we all have to face on this planet earth – the inevitability of the afterlife. If I had the power I'd make it compulsory reading for secondary schools.'

DR VICTOR ZAMMIT, LAWYER AND PSI RESEARCHER

'Emma Heathcote-James' latest book They Walk Among Us is a wealth of essential information and reference work concerning the vital subject of survival after physical death. All should read it.'

JAMES WEBSTER, WRITER, BROADCASTER AND AUTHOR OF
LIFE IS FOR EVER HAS SPENT 50 YEARS RESEARCHING THE CONTINUATION
OF LIFE FOLLOWING PHYSICAL DEATH

'This book presents the secular scientific case for survival after death – that the mind breaks away from the dead brain. This automatically brings into play a most important ethical code. "As you sow, so you will reap." There has to be perfect justice in the universe or we are all wasting our time trying to bring enlightenment to people on this backward planet.'

MICHAEL ROLL – THE CAMPAIGN FOR PHILOSOPHICAL FREEDOM AND
RESEARCHER, READING SURVIVAL AS A SECULAR SCIENTIFIC SUBJECT

'After Death Communication – *that's the title of a new book on spirit communication that will shortly be winging its way across the Atlantic... many have felt it best to keep these things to themselves for fear of being ridiculed or dismissed as indulging in wishful thinking. But why are people treated as odd for speaking of the experience asks Heathcote-James, if one in three of us has them?'*

'... *thoroughly researched and beautifully written with the scientific mind and lovingly spiritual heart of Emma Heathcote-James. It's a truly comforting book for those who've experienced an After Death Communication, and for those who wonder about life after death.'*

'*It's life's biggest mystery: Can we survive the grave? So why is science ignoring it?'*

ACKNOWLEDGEMENTS

*'One of the Greatest Pains to Human
Nature is the Pain of a New Idea'*

WALTER BAGEHOT

I WOULD LIKE TO RECOGNISE AND THANK all of the following people for their love, support and help, making both my life and this book possible.

First and foremost, to John Samson; thank you for unconditionally guiding, mentoring and teaching me the answers you have already found, thank you for reading through the various drafts as this book evolved and to Clare my thanks for supporting John in supporting me! The same to Michael Roll; thank you for your time, sharing your research and introducing me to so many others in the field – to Ron Pearson, Paul Read, Dr Victor Zammit, Dr Jeffrey Long and Jeff Rense, Professor Peter Wadhams and Professor Brian Josephson; many thanks for letting me use your personal findings and explaining them to me. To Tom Harrison, Veronica and the late Montague Keen, Rory McQuisten, Alan Cleaver, Gwen Byrne, the late Pat Jefferies, Linda and Carl Kimble – and all the others listed within these pages – I thank you for your time, support and help.

Thanks to the Society for Psychical Research, Marianne Rankin and Robert Waite and The Alistair Hardy Trust; the College for Psychic Studies, Julian Drewett, Val Baker and the Churches Fellowship for Psychical and Spiritual Studies, The SNU, Tony Ortzen and *Psychic News*, George Cranley and the Noah's Ark Society.

To David Thompson and in turn to William and Jack, I acknowledge and thank you for introducing me initially to something I never thought I would see, let alone understand. Also to Karl Fallon and Paul Barker, I thank you both especially for helping me with the terminology and goings-on and to Paul especially for your friendship.

To the various mediums, circles and sitters I have met and worked with as this book has evolved. For obvious reasons, I will not name you in person, but you each know who you are, thank you for all sharing, involving and writing this with me. To Rita Lorraine for appearing at the last minute – it's been a privilege to converse at last.

I acknowledge that without everyone's time, knowledge and support, this book wouldn't have been possible – it is far more a collaboration of their work than it is mine.

Next, I am extremely appreciative and thankful to each of the following special ladies who, individually and unknown to the others, have formed a strong support network and vital part of my life as I developed my work on this topic. Firstly, to Victoria Piechowiak, thank you for properly introducing me to Jung, for listening, helping me pick up and make sense of the pieces and for enabling me to find it from within to put them back together to make a clearer and better picture. To Dr Amanda Swindlehurst and Diana Harris, I thank you both for your wisdom, care and time when I needed it most. To Jaki Allen and Linda Meads, for sharing and teaching me again what I have learned to forget. To my fellow writer friends, Teresa Moorey, Glennyce Eckersley, Doreen Virtue, Kate Boydell, and Marilynne Lynn Berry, for watching from the sidelines and contributing words of reassurance and for your genuine understanding of the rollercoaster ride that producing a manuscript involves!

To my family and friends, primarily to Hector and Mr Mutley for curling up at my side as I wrote and dragging me through the fields each day! Thank you for being the most wonderful, consistent and faithful chaps in my life and for your companionship and unconditional love. To my parents and Dix for your love, care, support and persistence in putting up with me and thank you to Andy Weekes, the Middletons and the Baylisses for putting up with them! To those closer to home, especially Rob and Helen Davies, Su and Jim Appleby, Nick and Shell Wheatley, John Bluck, Nigel Stubbings, Hazel and Rod Attwood and, of course, Henry Appleby; thank you all for listening and caring enough to pull me out of my cave for much needed coffees, dog walks, glasses of wine, dinners and long evenings in front of the fire – you are all such incredibly special neighbours and I am so glad you're all a part of my life.

Thanks to Gordon Morris for introducing me to Shepherd's Fold; to Terry and Maureen Booth, Steve, Mr Darcy and all the beaters, shooters and doggies who lighten our wintry Wednesdays with such a welcome escape! Also, to my closest friends, especially John-Francis Friendship, Dan Howard, Collette Coll, Emma McIvor, Lavinia Smith-Lewis, Alix West, Gay Pilgrim, Sir Tim Ackroyd, Kathy Carmichael, Sarah Walker and the cast and crew of *Almost Strangers*, Kate and Richard Miles and Tess Loftus. I thank each of you for your continued friendship, fun, laughter and under-standing my mania throughout another book. Thank you for always being there when I needed you, and equally so for keeping out of the way when I didn't! I adore you all.

Finally, as ever, thanks in abundance to John Blake and Rosie Ries, Ailsa Macalister, Stuart Booth, Michelle Signore, Lucian Randall and all at Metro Publishing for believing in me yet again – and enabling yet another niche topic to be accessible to everyone.

FOREWORD

THROUGHOUT HUMAN HISTORY the problem of
whether we survive death has been the one of the most
pressing personal questions facing human beings. Children
and young people may imagine that they will live forever, but
as a person grows older the inevitability of approaching death
focuses the mind on the central question of survival. The
association of the mind and personality with brain function
and the certainty of the decay of the body, including the
brain, after death gives us logical reason to fear that death is
indeed the end.

Something inside many people rebels against this idea;
something tells them that their personality is unique and
indestructible and surely must continue in some form
beyond death. The big question is whether this is a real and
true feeling or whether the sense of self-consciousness that
we, as human beings, have developed through the growth of
our brains is cruelly deceiving us about our future.

In past times, man sought a solution to this problem through religion. The religious urge in man could be said to be due, in part, to a fear of death and a desire to believe in some authority, power or system that denies that death is the end and that tells us exactly what will happen after death and how we can achieve an optimum post-mortem state.

With the advent of systematic psychical research as a scientific subject in the late 19th century, the question of survival of death was subsumed into the overall problem of understanding psi. Early psychical researchers, who carefully investigated telepathy, precognition, psychokinesis and other psi phenomena, had, as an unspoken agenda, the idea that if psi between living beings could be demonstrated to be real, then this would also provide a mechanism by which disembodied entities could communicate, both with each other (so that continued experience and development are possible after death) and with living beings (via mediums, for example).

But a few brave researchers took the view that investigation of psychic phenomena is an indirect way of studying the problem of survival. Why not study the problem directly? It is, after all, a valid scientific question, and not necessarily a religious one at all. If it possible to survive death, then survival must be a natural phenomenon like any other, with laws and mechanisms by which the contents of one's mind and personality are retained in existence in some new form, which in principle can be discovered. Such research is fraught with difficulties, because nobody can be completely dispassionate about the subject to the extent that is desirable for a proper scientific investigation. Everyone has a personal agenda, either a will to believe or an indignant rejection of belief. Survival researchers need a superhuman degree of detachment.

They Walk Among Us

In *They Walk Among Us*, the areas in which scientific evidence of survival has been obtained are described. They are quite varied: mediumship, cross-correspondences, investigation of children who remember past lives and near death experiences. In many cases, when fraud is excluded, the only possible explanations for information received from the apparent surviving entity are genuine survival or a complicated structure of exceptional psi abilities, not normally displayed in other contexts. This is the super-ESP hypothesis. The jury is still out on what are the limits to ESP and whether they allow the super-ESP hypothesis to be accepted.

Much more research is needed, and it is ironic that this, the most important scientific question of all, has the fewest people working on it and the least (that is, zero) support from scientific funding agencies. But this should not deter the ingenuity of those who genuinely care about establishing whether we have a long-term future of which our material life is but one phase, or whether this life is all and that we must get used to the idea of our own mortality.

Professor Peter Wadhams, April 2007
Department of Applied Mathematics and Theoretical
Physics The University of Cambridge

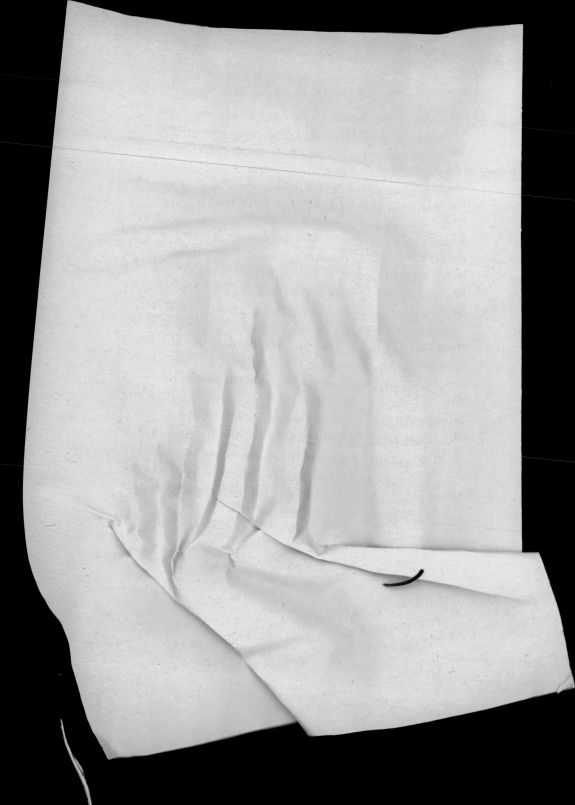

PREFACE

'The greatest adventure you can ever have is the exploration of your own consciousness. It is an adventure which makes any science-fiction story pale into insignificance until it looks like a nursery tale.'

DONALD PEAKE

The Secret of Genius
(Your Super Conscious Power)

MATERIALISATION AND PHYSICAL mediumship tends not to be a popular topic among the so-termed Mind, Body, Spirit publications. As I write, I have a very small pile of books beside me, and aside from Robin Foy's *In Pursuit of Physical Mediumship* and *The Scole Experiment,* there is little available to the lay reader or those coming to the topic for the first time. Other great books and accounts such as the feats of Jack Webber are all, sadly, out of print and a challenge to get hold of. For these reasons I wanted to explore the subject first-hand and meet with the relevant people.

Even as much as this 'unknown' territory scared me, I was still intrigued enough to continue the search. Fear of the unknown was my own stumbling block, and indeed one for those around me, too. It is something that each of us has to grapple with at some point. As human beings, we possess a greater consciousness and ability to think abstractly than any other living thing on this planet. Of course, much of the time this is an absolute blessing, but, as with all things, there is another side to it. It can also be a burden. At times, this ability to think and wonder, worry and question enables us to realise that we are each entirely alone in our own bodies. There is much we don't know or cannot comprehend, and this makes imperative the desire to have a belief structure or some form of spirituality in place – in order to understand the part we play in life.

From the early age of only ten years, the great pioneering psychologist Carl Jung began questioning such things and dedicated his life to trying to understand them. One only need read his *Memories, Dreams and Reflections* to see his reasoning and the struggle to achieve it.

Some of us, it seems are natural thinkers and ponderers, while others are content without the need or desire to know what life is all about. It is the people of the former orientation, those with a thirst for knowlege and truth, that I have been looking at and with whom I have been sharing experiences.

Surely, finding proof of these so common communications (be they through mediums or through, spontaneous, one-off After Death Communications – ADCs – as my last book explored) with those who have crossed over, is one of the most important discoveries in the history of human experience? Stripping away the materialism of the modern world, there are few things more important, vital or significant than the desire to know exactly who and what is our purpose of existence. In turn, this leads to the question of whether our loved ones, and indeed we ourselves, continue in some way, shape or form after we 'die'.

As we are caught up in the hustle and bustle of modern, day-to-day life, little thought is spared for our spirituality or to life's big questions. It feels as though we have gained scientific insight at the cost of losing our soul – something to which Jung referred on many occasions. Why is this book necessary today? Because I believe sincerely that it is a fact that we *need* modern science to account for and prove that materialisation phenomena exists – for without the science, sadly the occurrence is nothing. We have lost sight of the numinous – the science overrides it.

Still, underneath it all, I also believe most people are searching for meaning and truth in life. The root questions of: What am I? Who am I? What am I doing here? remain unanswered, many millennia from the time we first inhabited the planet. If we extend those questions to what happens when we die, we are confronted with seemingly unanswerable questions – such as: if a part of us survives death, how will we exist, and in what form? Is it possible that our soul or spirit continues to exist in another form for a long time – perhaps for thousands of years? In addition, how does time exist in the next dimension? Is there such a thing as time anyhow? Do we reincarnate and return in another shell to learn more of life's lessons until we are fully evolved as a human?

These are vital questions, and I struggle to believe that this current earthly life really is just all there is. It is interesting to note that practically every society in the world, in one way or another has beliefs in the continuing eternal existence of a part of us. A staggering 70 percent of the world's religions actually have reincarnation as their central core. This assertion of 'something' separating from the physical body and travelling to another world states that, in time, this something will return to reside in another physical body in order to evolve and learn more while living another life.

There are many theories, and many thought processes adhered to by many, but will we ever have 'the answer' that everyone on this planet can accept as being 'true'? Or, do we simply have to accept that there are some things in life we were born never to comprehend? After all, what would happen if we humans were able to account for and sum up life to the very last detail? Take for example the controversy that the cloning of living organisms – even people – has created. If we were able to recreate creation and play 'God', then what would happen? If we were suddenly able to answer all of the general 'what's it all about questioning' that afflicts us all at some point in our lives, what would result?

There are enormous consequences if all of these questions were ever to be answered. Nevertheless, I think as long as we tread this earth, there will be continuous attempts to find the answers.

Plato once stated that: 'the unexamined life is not worth living'. As much as ignorance is bliss, a great privilege is attached to searching within. There are many mysteries and wonders waiting to reveal themselves, but as for answers well, are there any?

Even if we think we have found them, how do we know they are correct? After all, perhaps there is a reason for the gaps in our understanding? Maybe we are unable to comprehend such things and part of our life is to understand our own reality? Look around: in essence, we are all alone in our own skin – we are all individual. We came into the world as individuals, but that did not worry or perplex us and each of us coped and survived the ordeal in one way or another. So, why is it so frightening to consider our departure from this world and having to leave it alone?

During our adult lives we grasp at external things to give our lives routine, structure and meaning to try and hold ourselves together. It is only when this is stripped back – be it through soul searching, depression or illness – that some people become aware of a different reality, a different state or perhaps something that is beyond them and the world in which they live.

Our televisions are crammed full of soap operas and documentaries; magazines and papers are littered with other people's lives; work can easily become the be all and end all. Yet surely, in essence, it is escapism, and an easier option, to close our minds and refuse to accept the possibility – rather than to look inward and examine our own lives. It is only when we are able to strip ourselves naked from our masks of a job, relationships or routine that we can ask: what exactly are we?

So, how did my journey bring me to the exploration of materialisation and the afterlife? My first book, *Seeing Angels*, came about after I unwittingly – and indeed, at the time unknowingly – carried out the UK's first university-based academic study that analysed contemporary accounts and testimonies of people who believed they had experienced some type of visitation by an angel. The research and its subsequent findings found its way into the national newspapers and to television and radio broadcasts and from it stemmed a documentary for the BBC television *Everyman* series, along with countless more magazine articles, radio and television slots and – finally – the book. From the eight hundred or so contributors I had found who attested to having been in an angelic presence, a small percentage attributed the angel identity to their own experiences of seeing deceased loved ones. Some of these ADCs were merely an audible familiar voice offering words of encouragement or reassurance that they were still there, watching over their living loved ones. Some were life-saving warnings or visions of times of crisis. Others were visions or feelings that the 'departed' were present. I included these few letters in one of the chapters and headed the section 'Granny as Your Guardian', outlining why they were so problematic for my research.

The words people choose to describe religious or numinous (spiritual) experiences present a fascinating area of discussion – and something my university work at the time particularly focused upon. Language is limited by its own vocabulary, with differing words conjuring up connotations we all take in different ways. I would argue that many words describe (essentially) the same experience; 'ghosts', 'spirits', 'guides', 'angels', 'guardian angels', 'energies'. All are theoretically separate entities, with their own dictionary definition, but describing one and the same thing[1]. The more I research this field, the more and more apparent this is becoming. To refine matters slightly: technically and traditionally speaking, angels and ghosts are separate entities; but from the sociological viewpoint, it was interesting how the terms and vocabulary were being merged. For the research back then, it was interesting that, these contributors were thinking of these ghostly apparitions as being angels, or in some case, their own guardian angel.

The other stumbling block was that many of these 'known' encounters could not be explained away as grief, mind projection or wishful thinking. I say this, because some provided messages, gleaning information which otherwise simply could not have been known. This aspect remains a definite sticking point for those people who are doing their utmost to destroy the very idea that we survive the death of our physical bodies. For example, I well remember being in the hospitality 'green room' before one television interview about the book and I was chatting to a well known psychologist who remains a regular in the media and whose only comeback to me, after exhausting the usual mind projection/crisis apparition theories and when confronted with a case that defied all explanation, was: 'Well, in cases like that, the recipients must be lying!' I am saddened by this type of reaction, for it tells me how this materialistic and physical world seems to have a need for explanations of everything to make us feel more secure and in control.

Within weeks of *Seeing Angels* being in the bookshops unsolicited testimonies & letters came flooding in. Yes, angels were at their peak; every Mind, Body, Spirit section of shelves was brimming with angel paraphernalia, yet, most interestingly, a large percentage of the letters grasped the few accounts I had outlined in that small 'Granny as your Guardian' section. Letters saying they'd had exactly the same thing; that they too had had a non-induced, one-off experience of seeing or hearing a deceased loved one. What was it all about? Were they alone? How common was it? Did I have any more information? But to me the publication of *Seeing Angels* had closed the cover on the research. I moved back into the media and was loving it. I had no plans to do any more academic research, let alone write any more. I sat on the letters until it became apparent I could no longer ignore their questions. There, among the accumulating pile of letters was the next book, *After Death Communication*.

So, it was from those few random letters amid the angel research that my interest into the afterlife was initially sparked and how research into ADC became incorporated into my work. It was at this time that I stumbled upon Bill and Judy Guggenheim's work in the USA, and their books *The ADC Project* and *Hello from Heaven*. They were doing the same with accounts of ADCs in the USA that I was doing with angel experiences in the UK. I got in touch and it was fantastic to know someone else was in the same boat as me – trying to tell the public that such experiences, despite rarely being discussed, were incredibly common and perfectly normal. As a result, and even more so than when I wrote the last book, I can now argue that perhaps they are. We now even have some of the science to explain it along the missing mathematics, as I shall explain later. So, it is really only now, after writing this book, that the whole concept seems only natural and normal to me, as opposed to being a tad quirky or way out.

The main thing which helped me in this understanding, and I hope helps you too, is this: 'Nothing happened yesterday in the laws of physics that does not happen today'. This is not some mad new gimmick, fad or phase. Materialisations are natural occurences, and explanations can only evolve through time and experience.

Consequently, I just hope this book complements the others already on offer and gives you, the reader a taste and can point you in the right direction if you want to explore things more.

A full glossary for the terms used in this book can be found on page 211.

INTRODUCTION –

STUMBLING UPON PHYSICAL MEDIUMSHIP AND MATERIALISATION PHENOMENA

'I was bold in the pursuit of knowledge, never fearing to follow truth and reason to whatever results they led.'

THOMAS JEFFERSON

IT WAS WHILE WRITING my previous book, that my interests widened from the one-off experiences I was reporting to looking for more concrete evidence that perhaps a part of us does indeed survive death. Naturally, through my work, I came into contact with academics, mediums and sitters. It was through these people that this book really fell into my lap.

Early on, I expressed concerns as to how my research has ended up homing in on ADC and the afterlife and that in my mid-twenties, ironically, I seemed to be spending more time thinking and writing about the plausibility of a next world than actually living in the current one! It was the closest thing I think one could call a spiritual crisis. So many of the things about which I was writing and thinking had no logical answers. Further, I didn't understand why they were so easily dismissed by science because they had never actually been 'disproved'. Through my curiosity, I was introduced to the topic of materialisation mediums and others who were investigating the phenomena.

I knew Michael Roll, founder of The Campaign for Philosophical Freedom, had taken part in repeatable experiments where he had physically met his father. His father died in 1967, but came back (materialised) in a solid form and embraced him at an experiment in 1983. Now, all scientists who have taken part in experiments where they have physically met people from the next world, agree that these etheric people are exactly the same as the people on earth and definitely are not angels, devils, gods or the 'big G' himself. Michael, along with many others, claimed our loved ones were still very much alive and now just operating in the invisible part of the universe. It was such a strong assertion and one that I was hearing again and again from many learned people. Was there something here I was missing out on? Was this really happening? If so, I asked, why on earth was it not public knowledge?

As much as I wanted to move into a new area of investigation, I was still absorbed and hungry to learn more. Such a phenomenon, if it truly existed, would provide us all with experimental proof that we do indeed survive death. It would prove every single account in my last book to be genuine and plausible, not wishful thinking of the bereaved, as has been theorised. Moreover, there was the enormous scientific and philosophical implications for us all if this physical phenomena was proven to be a natural force that had previously not been understood.

My degrees are in theology, for my passion has always been in religion and why people believe in certain structures and belief systems. Quirky religion has always been my thing; new age beliefs, witchcraft, cults, stigmata, visions and sightings. In fact, for some reason what is termed the 'paranormal' has always really excited and intrigued me. Yet, as a rationalist – though an open-minded one – I still found it incredibly hard to get my head around the fact that one could meet with the 'dead'.

It didn't help when I tried to explain the idea to others either. As with my other books, I was met with raised eyebrows and mumblings such as: 'Where on earth do you find these crackpots?' But – and the big but – what if these crack pots were all true? What if all the experiences had by people in my first and second books were natural and completely normal? What if such experiences could be explained scientifically? As indicated earlier, the idea scared me – but at the same time intrigued me. Thus began my next quest.

In the beginning, I tried to explain the concept of materialisation to my parents and friends. Granted, even to me, it sounded way out. The topic is even treated with suspicion by the mainstream media. Although physical mediumship is a little known area, it is a vast subject, and to try and put it across and explain it all in a ten-minute interview is completely impossible.

This is the one problem with the media. I know this from working in the industry and unless an hour-long documentary is devoted to this topic, bite-sized segments, whether a news bulletin or a guest slot on a show, are never going to give the phenomena the time it needs to be fully explained.

Proof at Last?

So, I began this new work along these lines: if I was to accept that this rarely talked about phenomenon *did* exist amid psychic circles, and *if* it *were* to be genuine, then somehow it had to have a rational explanation and be logical. In other words, scientists believe nothing is outside of nature's laws, so if something genuinely happens, then there must be a rational explanation to account for it. Indeed, to tie things in together, if the experiences of angels and ADC that I had collected were real, then all of these experiences also had to come within the laws of nature – they had to be answerable *scientifically*, through a branch of physics or mathematics as a natural philosophy.

To my shock and excitement, it didn't take long until I was told that it could be. A man called Ronald Pearson had done just this – provided the missing equations. Materialisation can be scientifically explained – or, as some would claim, is now proven. Subabtomic physics and the latest ideas within the study of quantam mechanics, along with Ronald Pearson's findings, quantified that reality does indeed exist beyond our five physical senses. Until now, from our ancient ancestors right through to present day, such experiences were thought to be 'supernatural' and outside the laws of nature but there is, at last, an explanation for materialisation (which in turn solves much more so-called 'paranormal' phenomena).

Mind Bending: Getting to Grips with a New Way of Thinking

It was desperately hard to take it all in. To accept that all of the so-called paranormal phenomena can now be *scientifically* explained. My biggest mind bender was the fact that for once the answer does not lie in religion – and how I hated myself for saying this: this phenomenon I had spent years exploring was now faltering before my very eyes. I will be honest; it made me ill. In the beginning, the whole thing was so vast that I felt I couldn't cope with it. It broke down everything I believed, and as much as I tried to write and research while sitting on the fence, I simply could not continue in that way. Everything I was absorbing just seemed to make so much sense. It soon became clear that the whole subject of life after death could indeed be explored more fully and scientifically by subatomic physics than religion or parapsychology – the topics which to date I had been immersed in, but admittedly had still not found any answers through.

As I dipped into the unknown, I experienced acute anxiety and stress for the first time in my life. The more I explored, learned and understood, the more alone, isolated and different I felt. For several months I became completely introverted, trying desperately to unscramble this big load of 'what ifs' that were circling my head. Why was I plagued with questioning, why couldn't I leave the topic and go and get a normal job? Friends and relations wanted me to drop this whole book idea and write about something easier. But I was in too deep, book or no book.

For me, the questions and yearning for the truth were already there, and whether I wrote this book or not, somehow I had to get my head around them and answer them for myself. I needed to understand what was going on, and I needed to re-address the 'biggies' of what we are, why we are here, and so forth. I was extremely privileged to have so many supportive people in my life and found myself surrounded by some really wise and learned people who had already been through the questioning that I had, along with years of research. In fact, it felt to me that some of them were put there especially, at just the right time.

It took me over a year to psyche myself up to agree to join in with one of these experiments, despite having been invited from the start. That process alone – finding and being accepted into one of the established and mature home circles – was fraught with its own problems. Aside from Alan Cleaver, a *Psychic News* journalist in the 1980s, I was the first 'outsider' writer to be accepted and admitted. I was, I think quite understandably, nervous about what I would see and find. What would happen if someone I knew appeared materialised in the room? Three people extremely close to me had all died within the past two years. Two of them had been cremated and the idea of being able to hold their hand again went against all the rational laws I had been taught. Those I'd so recently grieved knew of my interests, work and writing, so if anyone would come through to prove it existed, then surely it would be one of them? And then what? Well, it would go an awful long way in providing concrete personal evidence.

Then came my more apparent fear. What if they didn't appear and nothing happened? Although I was reassured that this was unlikely, it was still a worry. The spirit world, presuming it existed, couldn't really win either way! Then more anxieties crept in. How would I feel cooped up for several hours in a pitch black room with up to 20 other people, with no windows and the door tightly sealed with adhesive tape? I am not claustrophobic, but the thought of the setting made my heart race a little faster, as did the wondering if a relative of mine was to appear. How I would react? Would I be calm or would I freak out? If I freaked out, I was practically hermetically sealed in the room, panic attack or not. Would my professional hat remain intact or would I be a laughing stock? However, the bottom line was how could I write a book about something I wasn't even prepared to witness? My other books have merely reported, analysed and categorised other people's accounts. Never before has the opportunity been there to be able to induce such experiences. If I found that it was one big hoax, then that was that. However, if I could find no known rational explanation and if all these academics and others were correct in their findings, then what we were onto was something vast.

Then, just as things were going swimmingly well, the unexpected happened. The medium I was working alongside went cold on me, deciding only hours before a sitting that I could not go in with night-vision goggles (to check for fraud or trickery). He then explained that he was not as developed as perhaps I had previously understood.

So, three-quarters of the way through writing this book, I was circle-less, and alone. Should I close the covers, thinking the worst and wondering whether he was a fraud? (However, with the revision of this book and after meeting with him again last year in Australia and speaking about all of this, I can honestly clarify that this most definitely is not the case.) Were there any fully developed physical materialisation mediums around with whom experiments could take place? Should I carry on and see where the book took me? Needless to say, cocooned by many others, I chose the latter, deciding to write the book as I had my last two – not from personal experience, but through the experiences of others. I felt it necessary to really know the subject but still remain impartial. However, my writing of this is still very much from a different angle to other books on the market – for I am not a Spiritualist, nor am I on a religious crusade. No, I merely report the current situation as I experience it and with the input of people who literally have seen it!

The Next Step?

I expect many to close the book at this point and refuse to read on. As indicated already, I ignored the findings for almost six months before I dared to delve in and look closely.

It is difficult for us, as human beings, to fully understand the multi-dimensional world that I am sure the Universe really must be. Most often, we apprehend the reality as three- or four-dimensional. People who have raised their energy to a higher level may be able to apprehend a couple or more dimensions but, even so, those dimensions are just a small part of all the dimensions that really exist.

I have experienced trance sittings and seen countless messages conveyed by clairaudients, clairsentients and clairvoyants. Such phenomena, in themselves, intrigued me, as did independent direct voice. Yet, as a sceptic, and like most others, I was aware of the ambiguity and scant messages often received – though I did appreciate there was something going on which was beyond us. However, to then take that one step on and to find out that some mediums have matured to the extent they can not just see or hear the deceased themselves, but can actually enable the person to return in full view of the other sitters and impart messages and reminiscences is pretty astounding, mind-bending stuff.

I heard stories of fully materialised relatives, friends and guides having returned to independent sitters (as opposed to regular circle members) that I had been talking with. I heard reports that they had witnessed a solid drumstick being pushed through the centre of a table, a chair dematerialising and reappearing in the next room, and deceased relatives and loved ones appearing before all their eyes. All these defied logic. Or rather, logic as I understood it. It alarmed me; it frightened me. Not because I thought it was absolute poppycock, but because I wondered about the implications if it were true.

Very little is written on the topic of physical phenomena or materialisation and very few people outside Spiritualist and 'paranormal' investigative circles know about it. This is something I want desperately to change.

In the UK, at the time of writing, the number of materialisation mediums can just about be counted on one hand and, of these, the majority are developing. Another reason why physical mediumship is not known about by many people is due largely to the poor treatment of materialisation mediums by ill-meaning researchers after the 1950s. It was this that drove physical mediumship underground, with physical mediums in the West tending to only sit for friends and relatives behind closed doors. However, in 1990, The Noah's Ark Society for Physical Mediumship was founded to provide a safe haven for mediums from what it terms: 'The harsh treatment meted out to early pioneer physical mediums from so-called researchers, who insisted on trussing up the medium, demanding endless tests, and inflicting grave harm physically through violating the laws governing physical phenomena[1].' At the time of writing this book (March 2004), its membership consists of over 500 people spread throughout 21 different counties.

Of course, there are millions of genuine seekers of knowledge and the truth who would give their back teeth to meet people from the etheric realms or wavelengths. However, I do need to stress that such important experiments and séances must not be used as a peep show. I am confident that very soon, scientific reports will be brought into the open and break through the barriers of suppression that are erected at the moment. I say this on behalf of one far lesser known circle that has been practising physical closed circles with astonishing results since 1990.

My early fears while writing have been that publicising these people's unique gifts would make everyone want a piece of them; and the risk is still there. However, they all know about this book and I have maintained their anonymity. Physical sittings are booked months ahead and, because of the risk to the medium, guests are carefully chosen.

The layperson only need pick up a copy of *Psychic News* or subscribe to one of the many journals to read reports of occurrences and events, and to realise the number of groups and societies who incorporate this form of mediumship into their research.

1

EXPLORING THE PROOF
OF AN AFTERLIFE

'There is one thing stronger than all the armies of the world, and that is an idea whose time has come.'

VOLTAIRE

APPARITIONS AND VISIONS of deceased loved ones being seen again, long after their physical bodies had been buried or cremated, are among the oldest and most common type of paranormal phenomena – and of course was the theme my last book, *After Death Communication*, dealt with exclusively. The notion of an afterlife and stories of ghostly sightings have been circling around as long as the human race has inhabited the earth. This preoccupation with the next world, and longing for confirmation that our loved ones have lived on – and are able somehow to communicate that fact to us – has become an integral part of many people's lives. Yet, is still treated with suspicion and taboo.

Today, we are living in an age of science, an age where

many people are inclined to accept the truth of anything only by observation and experiment, rather than by mere belief. With the most recent scientific advances, it seems as though we are becoming even more rationalistic in outlook, with blind belief fast disappearing. However, science does not have to be something to fear. Indeed, in some instances, especially in its latest fields of research into the so-called 'theory of everything', it can even back up that 'blind belief' with which so many of us have struggled.

Death and dying are among the few things beyond our control and a reality that unites us as human beings. It is one of the undisputable facts of life – one which we cannot escape and one which ignites questions within us all. What is going to happen the moment our heart takes its last beat and we exhale our final breath? Do we simply cease to exist or do we pass quite naturally into another dimension?

I consider that there is evidence in abundance for the latter. There are many, many testimonies of loved ones returning from beyond the grave, and reports of near death experiences, of astral travel, past lives and out-of-body experiences are commonplace. Furthermore, there are many commonalities linking these phenomena together. Throughout the 20th century, some of the most intelligent and brilliant scientists made significant contributions to the study of life after death. In so doing, many used science, which, in a nutshell, seems to concede that the empirical evidence for the afterlife is irrefutable.

Assertions of surviving physical death also form the fundamental basis of Christianity and are a huge factor in all the other major world religions and belief systems. Many sacred texts talk about a person appearing and disappearing in front of a crowd. Indeed, such is the case with the Bible's accounts of Jesus. Investigators call the appearance and disappearance of people and things 'materialisation' and 'dematerialisation'.

What of Traditional Science?

In the last few years, the great debate of human consciousness has circled ever more fiercely. To some there appears general consensus that Einstein could have been wrong with his theory of relativity – meaning the Big Bang theory could in no way be valid. Equally, at the subatomic level and in fields of quantum physics, there has seemed to be conflict between the science of astrophysics and the behaviour of the universe on the cosmic scale.

Interestingly, both of these orthodox scientific teachings begin with the clear-cut assumption that death is the end of everything – the mind dies with the brain, as the mind and brain are one and the same. However, the evidence now points to the opposite. The mind and brain are not one but two differing entities. It is a little known fact that for over a hundred years we have actually had experimental scientific proof that we all survive the death of our physical bodies that the living mind separates from the dead brain. Furthermore, there is now a vast amount of work being carried out to try and link the macro and sub-micro scales of the nature and behaviour of matter – with so-called 'string theory' being postulated as the 'theory of everything'. Most of the conclusions do not now conflict with what once might have been called the 'paranormal', or the strangeness of the human mind.

I use the term 'mind', as some do indeed refer to this part

of us as being the mind, others call it the personality, consciousness, aura, spirit or the soul. However, to try to avoid confusion, I shall refer to it hereon as the etheric body – the part of us that lives on after death. On a popularised level, we have all encountered testimonies of Near Death Experiences (NDE) where a person who has been clinically dead on the operating slab has come back to life and can recount an entire conversation that was held, having witnessed it in their 'phantom' body from above. It is precisely this that I am talking about. If we begin from the premise that the mind and brain are separate, and that a part somehow continues, then it seems to me that so many so-called paranormal experiences and questions can be answered. If we can grasp hold of this idea alone, a whole new world of potential opens. Indeed, I think that this separate entity, whatever tag you ascribe to it, lives on after our body (our shell) dies. Also, the more I look into it, the more I read and the more people I converse with, the more the evidence and the backing seems to be in place.

The Big Bang theory is currently the dominant scientific explanation for the origin of the universe and what we all are. According to Big Bang', the universe was created between 10 billion and 20 billion years ago from a cosmic explosion that hurled matter in all directions.

In 1927, the Belgian priest Georges Lemaître was the first to propose that the universe began with the explosion of a primeval atom. His proposal came after applying the red shift in light from distant nebulae, as observed and recorded by astronomers, to a model of the universe based on relativity. Years later, the astronomer Edwin Hubble found experimental evidence to help justify Lemaître's theory. He found that distant galaxies in every direction are going away from us at speeds proportional to their distance. The Big Bang was initially suggested because it explains why distant galaxies are travelling away from us at great speeds. The theory also predicts the existence of cosmic background radiation (the glow left over from the explosion itself). The Big Bang Theory received its strongest confirmation when this radiation was discovered in 1964 by Arno Penzias and Robert Wilson, who later won the Nobel Prize for their work.

Although the Big Bang theory is widely accepted, it most probably will never be proved; consequently, it leaves a number of tough, unanswered questions. Only very recently dark energy was discovered; this seems to be making the universe expand faster and faster, rather than more and more slowly, as was previously thought. Yet, whatever the outcome of the research and also of the newest work at the other end of the scale of matter, the subatomic, the need for another theory is back in the offing.

Some Wise People

Now, other far more illustrious pens than mine have experimented with and written about this subject; and many of the people who have assisted me while writing this have spent vast numbers of years enquiring into it. I cannot profess to ever being able to acquire the knowledge and expertise they all share, and I need to make this clear from the start. Therefore, from the outset and having recorded my grateful thanks in the Acknowledgments, I want to introduce you to the people who have been paramount in this book's evolution.

First, John Samson, a member of the Society for Psychical Research who has been beside me every step of the way and whose wise words and learned brain have enabled me to (just about!) keep my feet on the ground. As you will read, the findings I have had to grapple are an awful lot to take in.

Next, if it wasn't for the support and years of dedicated research conducted by Michael Roll, who I see as the central axis of this book, I would never have been introduced to, or become interested in materialisation.

Several mediums have patiently explained everything I have written about. Never before have I had the opportunity to read findings of such visions induced and replicated and then explained scientifically as being a natural phenomenon (from hereon, think 'super-normal' rather than 'para-normal') and as for the explanations, I thank Professor Peter Wadhams, a physicist from Cambridge University, who has openly backed the experiments carried out by Sir William Crookes. Rita Lorraine (who was also known as Rita Goold) and others who also start from the base that the mind and brain are separate.

Finally, to Ronald Pearson, who in 1988 came up with the missing theory that seems to exactly match the past experiments. I feel so privileged to have worked alongside them all and I just hope I have done justice to all their work and findings and that they each, individually, get the recognition that they so rightly deserve.

Collating Knowledge and Experience
I see my role as a spokesperson for these people, a vehicle in which all of the knowledge to date can be collected

together in one volume and brought out into the public arena rather than being hidden amid the walls of academia. Personally, I think each and every one of us has a right to know about it and therefore I want to get through the barriers and make this knowledge accessible to all. What use is it hidden? It affects us all and ultimately the way we live and use our time on earth.

At some time in our lives, be it after a family bereavement or amid a personal crisis, we will all ask ourselves the question: 'What will happen to me when I die?' The religion of Spiritualism affirms that the human spirit survives physical death and enters a spirit world, which surrounds and interpenetrates our material life. It asserts that the truth of this belief can be demonstrated under the right conditions, when communication can (and does) take place between the worlds of spirit and earthly being, and that this communication is only possible through individuals who have what are known as mediumistic abilities and who are known as mediums. However, we can now go one step further, even so far as to take 'religion' out of the equation, and insert potential 'knowledge' by saying we can scientifically prove it as fact. In other words, we are now able to explain scientifically and logically how we live on and, indeed, how the two worlds can and do interact.

As far as I am aware, an agreement has never been reached as to whether entities seen amid an ADC experience or in visions of 'ghosts' are real material forms (which somehow becomes incorporated into our reality) or are just some kind of weird hallucination. Of course, the bigoted sceptics argue the latter, but since researching my first two books and looking into recent scientific findings, I now feel armed and able to argue confidently as to the former. My first defence of this statement comes from little-known repeatable experiments, which were carried out (and, indeed, are still going on) and are able to induce such experiences in a séance sitting with a special type of medium.

There are many credible documented accounts of full and partial materialisations of known deceased people and animals, objects and sitters being levitated, the apportation of flowers, coins and other objects, and detailed and specific information coming from the mouths of those who have passed on. Such goings-on happen within the branch of physical mediumship, which is a very, very rare gift. It has been estimated that only one in 100,000 people has the ability to develop it and it generally takes 20 years or so of disciplined effort to do so[2]. However, in some instances the reverse is also true, the Midlands-based medium Rita Lorraine was born with the right chemical make up and developed very quickly (see Chapter 8).

Physical mediumship producing materialisations is currently the *only* phenomenon able to provide experimental proof of survival after death. What I am most interested in is the fact that during the physical séances (for which I use the term 'experiment') these rare mediums are able to bring the deceased back to earth in solid form. All of the assembled room is able to see, touch, speak with and hold their deceased loved ones.

Any scientist will tell you that if we want to study anything which is beyond our five physical senses we need to work with an instrument. We can't see microbes without a microscope or television signals without a television set. At the moment, the only way we can see, hear, smell, or touch people in the invisible part of the universe is by inducing the phenomena by working with a physical medium. Of course, one can communicate via clairvoyants or trance mediums, but not in the way they themselves can communicate using their own five senses – to see the deceased in solid form and talk and touch directly with them. Other one-off spontaneous ADC's happen too, without the need for a 3rd party, but these experiences seem to occur via the loved one making the effort to come back.

This book focuses on us being able to regain that link, and this explains ADC, ghost sightings, & all paranormal phenomena as a result.

2

Mediums, Physical Phenomena and Materialisations: the Pioneers

IN MY PREVIOUS BOOKS, I spoke of a shift in awareness and I maintain that we are still moving into a far more spiritual and less religious dimension. However, it is important to recognise the work of earlier investigators prepared to stick by their findings and beliefs in the face of the established scene at the time. So, let us take a step back into the fairly recent past. Mediumship and séances were originally popularised in the first half of the 20th century and concentrated on producing physical results. The Fox sisters gave early demonstrations of sounds coming from the walls and floor. Initial investigations were unable to find a logical explanation for these noises. The sisters were further investigated and tested. On one occasion, they were made to stand on tables covered with feather pillows with their skirts tied above their ankles. Still the rapping noises were heard, and once again no logical explanation could be found. As their mediumship continued, other unexplained events were noticed including objects moving, heavy tables levitating and hands and faces appearing.

In these early days, events such as table-tilting became quite popular. This often involved a group of people sitting around a table calling out letters of the alphabet waiting for the table to tilt when a correct letter was reached. It was a slow and cumbersome method and easily faked by fraudulent mediums. Yet even so, some excellent evidence was and can be achieved.

Daniel Dunglas Home

Despite the above, it was perhaps the extraordinary talents of Daniel Dunglas Home that did most to bring spiritualism to the recognition of the general public. Home was a physical medium, born in Scotland and raised in the USA. For 20 years between 1854 and 1874, he gave séances for friends and acquaintances in England and Europe, refusing to take payment for his services.

The extraordinary thing about Home was that he was able to work in daylight or gaslight and in houses he had never been in before. Under these circumstances, materialised forms were often seen around him. Disembodied hands would appear, allowing sitters to inspect them, touch them and shake them – but if anybody tried to cling onto them they melted away. He was also well known for his feats of levitation, and during his séances it was reported his chair would rise from the floor while he was still seated in it.

Towards the end of his career, Home was asked to demonstrate his powers in laboratory trials. In tests by Alexander von Boutlerow in Russia and by Sir William Crookes in England, he was able to produce telekinetic effects at a distance and these could be measured on weighing machines. Séances were attended by members of the aristocracy, literary giants and eminent scientists like Alfred Russel Wallace and Francis Galton. It is said that: 'Famous conjurers, too, came to his séances hoping to be able to catch him out, but they all went away disappointed.' In all that time, cheating was never detected despite him being one of the best-known men in Europe.

William Crookes and Oliver Lodge

The late scientist Sir William Crookes, who had worked & experimented with Dunglas Home, was fascinated with research and experiments surrounding the afterlife. In 1874, he was able to prove all his theories about the mind and brain being separate by carrying out incredible repeatable experiments in laboratory conditions with a physical medium called Florence Cook. Each time Florence gave a demonstration in his strict laboratory conditions, a person from the invisible part of the universe materialised, in solid form. His results were published in the *Quarterly Journal of Science* in 1874.

Following this revolutionary discovery, Crookes was knighted, made President of the Royal Society, and King Edward VII presented him with the highest decoration in the land – The Order of Merit.

Crookes believed completely that these findings finally

proved that there was life after death – and went on in 1882 to found the Society for Psychical Research (SPR) in order to carry on this vital work with mediums. Such experiments, proving survival beyond death, were subsequently repeated by international teams of scientists: The Nobel Laureate for Medical Science, Professor Charles Richet (French team); Professor Schrenck Notzing (German team); Dr Glen Hamilton (Canadian team); and Dr W.J. Crawford (Irish team).

Many recent discoveries, including the theories of Ron Pearson (see Chapters 10 and 11) confirm time and time again that Sir William Crookes was correct in his conclusions. However, at the time, smear campaigns resulted in him being called a liar, cheat, crank, a fraud or a sex maniac and were surely initiated simply to mask his uncomfortable discoveries. His only 'crime', it seems, was to tell the truth. When criticised by Carpenter in the *Quarterly Journal of Science*, he gave the following reply, which in itself speaks of the achievements and credibility of himself as a scientist:

'My greatest crime seems to be that I am a 'specialist of specialists'. It is indeed news to me that I have confined my attention only to one special subject. Will my reviewer kindly say what that subject is? Is it General Chemistry, whose chronicler I have been since the commencement of the Chemical News in 1859? Is it Thallium, about which the public have probably heard as much as they care for? Is it Chemical Analysis, in which my recently published Select Methods are the result of twelve years work?

Is it disinfections and the 'Prevention and Cure of Cattle Plague', my published report on which may be said to have popularised Carbolic Acid? Is it Photography, on the theory and practice of which my papers have been very numerous? Is it metallurgy of gold and silver, in which my discovery of the value of sodium in the amalgamation process in now largely used in Australia, California and South America?

Is it Physical Optics, in which department I have space only to refer to papers of some Phenomena of Polarised Light, published before I was twenty one; to my detailed description of the Spectroscope and labours with this instrument, when it was almost unknown in England; to my papers on the Solar and Terrestrial Spectra; to my examination of the Optical Phenomena of Opals, and construction of the Spectrum Microscope; to my papers on the Luminous Intensity of Light; and my description of my Polarization Photometer?

Or is it my speciality Astronomy and Meteorology, in as much as I was for twelve months at the Radcliffe Observatory, Oxford, where, in addition to my principal employment of arranging the meteorological department, I divided my leisure between Homer and Mathematics at Magdalen Hall, planet-hunting and transit tracking with Mr Pogson, now Principal of the Madras Observatory, and celestial photography with the magnificent heliometer attached to the Observatory? My photographs of the Moon, taken in 1855, at Mr Hartnup's Observatory, Liverpool, were for years the best extant, and I was honoured by a money grant from the Royal Society to carry out further work in connection with them. These facts, together with my trip to Oran last year, as one of the Government Eclipse Expedition, and the invitation recently received to visit Ceylon for the same purpose, would almost seem to show that Astronomy was my speciality. In truth, few scientific people are less open to the charge of being a 'specialist of specialists'.

As for Sir Oliver Lodge, he was the first person to transmit a message by radio – on 14 August 1894. The physics laboratory at Liverpool University is named after him. Yet Lodge's contribution to radio has been played down and the reason is surely and solely because he also dared to say that 'paranormal' phenomena are, in fact, a branch of physics.

It seems to me that there is almost certainly a conspiracy to try to suppress the uncomfortable discoveries in science around those who appear to support the 'unexplained'. Perhaps because such findings seem to have repercussions in many different areas…?

First, there are the many religionists fighting to defend their faiths – or as some might put it, 'to keep their monopoly on the life after death industry'.

Then, there are the 'pseudo-scientists', fighting to keep their power structures intact – a reaction perhaps best summarised by Adrian Berry the Science Correspondent of the *Daily Telegraph*, when he wrote: 'Few subjects more infuriate scientists than claims of paranormal phenomena because, if confirmed, the whole fabric of science would be threatened.'

I find it absurd that such exciting scientific discoveries are kept away from the attention of the general public. Many scientists still seem to shy away from supporting the work of William Crookes and Oliver Lodge – even in the press and on every radio and television programme that is made on the so-called paranormal.

Why, if Crookes' work was such a revolutionary discovery in physics, did it fail to have the impact that it should have done? It should have been headline news splashed across the world. The main problem was that the 'dead' person, Katie King, who materialised from the etheric world, had died so long ago that Sir William Crookes was unable to get living friends and relations to take part in his repeatable experiments. However, such experiments, in which a daughter was reunited with her 'dead' mother and several parents with their 'dead' children, have since been replicated (see Chapter 8).

The other problem faced by Crookes was that although phenomenal, the experiments lacked the mathematical theory to back up what was being observed. But thanks to recent exciting discoveries in subatomic physics, the study of the invisible part of the universe, and the published work of Ronald Pearson, I believe we now have the missing mathematical theory that matches Crookes' (and subsequent) pioneering experiments.

Carmine Mirabelli

Evidence for materialisation is substantive not only in England and the United States but also in other countries. David Ash and Peter Hewitt's book, *The Vortex* (1994), talks about Carmine Mirabelli's (1889–1950) mediumship in Brazil. In 1927, a book entitled *O Medium Mirabelli* contained a 74-page account of phenomena that occurred – in broad daylight at times – in the presence of up to 60 witnesses. Many of these witnesses were representatives of the leading scientific and social circles of Brazil, and among those who gave their names were the President of Brazil, the Secretary of State, two professors of medicine, 72 doctors, 12 engineers, 36 lawyers, 89 men of public office, 25 military men, 52 bankers, 128 merchants and 22 dentists as well as members of religious orders[1].

The testimony of so many prominent credible witnesses could not – and still cannot – easily be overlooked. Consequently, a Brazilian committee of 20 leading figures was created and headed by the President, to interview witnesses and to decide what should be done scientifically to investigate Mirabelli's powers. In 1927, the committee decided to mount a series of controlled investigations by the newly established Academia de Estudos Psychicos using controls followed by European mediums[2].

At one of the séance experiments conducted in the morning in full daylight in the laboratory of the investigating committee and in front of many people of note, including 10 men holding the degree of Doctor of Science, the form of a little girl materialised beside the medium. Dr Ganymede de Souza, who was present, confirmed that the child was his daughter who had died a few months before and that she was wearing the dress in which she had been buried. Another observer, Colonel Octavio Viana, also took the child in his arms, felt her pulse and asked her several questions, which she answered with understanding. Photographs of the apparition were taken and appended to the investigating committee's report. The child then floated around in the air and disappeared, after having been visible in daylight for 36 minutes. The form of Bishop Jose de Camargo Barros, who had recently lost his life in a shipwreck, also appeared in full insignia of office. He conversed with those present and allowed them to examine his heart, gums, abdomen and fingers before disappearing.

At 3.30pm, another séance was conducted at Santos; 60 witnesses attested their signatures to the report of what had happened. The deceased Dr Bezerra de Meneses, an eminent hospital physician, materialised and spoke to all of the assembled witnesses to assure them that it was himself. His voice was carried all over the room via a megaphone and several photographs were taken of him. For 15 minutes, two doctors, who had known him in life, examined him and announced that he was an anatomically normal human being before he shook hands with the spectators. Finally, he rose into the air and began to dematerialise, his feet vanishing first, followed by his legs and abdomen, chest, arms and, last of all, head. After the apparition had dematerialised, Mirabelli was found to be still tied securely to his chair and seals were intact on all the doors and windows. The photographs accompanying the report show Mirabelli and the apparition on the same photographic plate.

At another séance experiment under controlled conditions, Mirabelli himself dematerialised to be found later in another room. Yet, the seals put upon his bonds were intact as were the seals on the doors and windows of the séance room[3]. The materialisations took place in daylight in the presence of hundreds of hardcore sceptics and scientists. and it is noteworthy that none have so far been rebutted, nor are they likely to be.

Many great physical mediums over the past hundred or so years have been documented – if you are interested in reading more about the history I suggest you begin with those such as Florence Cook, Jack Webber[4], Helen Duncan, Minnie Harrison and Alec Harris.

Alec Harris

Alec Harris is worth mentioning here as he was a former sceptic about psychic matters, but soon became one of the world's most brilliant materialisation mediums. Alec only spoke English, but etheric communicators spoke through him in various different languages. On one occasion, Ghandi materialised and spoke with an eminent medical man in Hindi. Another time, a professional illusionist sat with him and had his 'dead' father appear, and among other evidence, he used a pet name known only to the sitter's family. There are reports of so many as 30 materialisations occurring amid two-and-a-half-hour sittings. (Later in this book Chapter 8 is a report from someone who was fortunate to have sat personally with Alec and his wife Louie in Johannesburg, and it is interesting to link it with the following reports that I have taken from Louie's book, which she wrote after his death in 1974[5].)

The landmark stage in Alec's mediumship came in 1940, when it became clear that the circle would soon enjoy the company of materialisations and members decided to meet for this purpose. On the first occasion, it was reported: 'To our amazement a luminous ball began forming in the centre of the cabinet curtain. A face could be seen[6].'

This was followed by similar occurrences. It was apparent that having obtained the initial stages of materialisations, much more work needed to be done. Louie recorded: 'As the weeks went by, the figures grew stronger and stronger. The sitters were delighted to see Connie materialising.' Eventually, the coming of the 'dead' in material form was a common feature and Louie noted: 'Now, I began to understand about the "great work" it was said we had to perform. I envisaged the enormous possibilities this type of mediumship would provide for helping the bereaved[7].'

As had occurred in the First World War, many mediums were able to bring comfort to the bereaved by demonstrating the survival of those slaughtered in the Second World War. Alec was one such medium.

During these years, a woman was noticed at a local Spiritualist church looking very strained, and Louie became aware of the presence of a young soldier doing his utmost, albeit unsuccessfully, to make himself known to her. Therefore, it was suggested that the woman attend the next meeting of Alec's circle. She arrived and Louie placed her in the front row near to the cabinet. Shortly after the séance began, a young man left the cabinet and held out his arms to the woman, saying: 'Mum, it's Derry'. She gave an anguished cry, jumped from her seat and went to the boy. He put his arms around her. The mother broke down and wept unrestrainedly in her 'dead' son's arms. Gently, he comforted his mother, saying he was always with her. Then he changed the subject quite unexpectedly by remarking: 'I want you to be quite sure this is really me. Look, I've still got it.' The solid form took her hand and placed it on his chest. 'Can you feel it Mum?' he asked[8]. Later, they learned the boy had had a deformed breast bone which his family had laughingly called his 'chicken bone'. To give his mother positive proof of his identity, the son had materialised with the same physical deformity from which he had suffered before his death.

The Formula

What was achieved by the investigation committee dealing with Mirabelli, by Crookes dealing with Florence Cook and countless other investigators in the field with their repeatable experiments on such mediums was phenomenal. However, although their experiments and findings proved that all this happened, what was still missing were the mathematic formulas to explain it logically and back up the findings.

Since then, many have tried to come up with the missing link and it is only now that a formula has come close to explaining it scientifically – one which not only works, but logically explains the fact that something lives on and is able to materialise of its own accord, not just through spontaneous ADC visions and ghost sightings, but also special mediums during experimental settings. Indeed, I believe Ronald Pearson has come the closest so far to provide us with this missing link. We *know* these things happen but, until now, there was not the science to explain why. Pearson's theory and formulae report that materialisations, whether they are induced by a physical medium or are spontaneous ghostly sightings or visions, simply cannot be figments of the imagination.

It was only because of the lack of science that sceptics had their day. Let's see how they argue now…

3

DEATH AND THE AFTERLIFE: SCIENCE AND RELIGION

*'Grief is healing. To take away our grief is to take away
our healing. And learning about life after death helps us heal
with greater hope, comfort and peace.'*

BOB OLSON

MOST PEOPLE FEAR death; not just the manner in which they will die, but what will become of them when they do. It is this question of fear, which affects every one of us, even those who claim to believe in a life after death, and it all goes back to the difference between believing and knowing. It is all well and good to believe, but what if they are wrong? What if, when it comes to it, there is no life after death? Alternatively, perhaps there is, but what if for some reason or other one doesn't make it?

I would define death in terms of being that point when the immortal part of us – that awareness, that thinking, feeling part of us which is the 'real' us – departs from the physical body and severs most of its links with it. It is when the living part of us ceases to activate the physical body. In the moments preceding death the physical body starts to break down. But what happens to the spirit or soul?

All these questions engage the mind of each of us at some point in our lives. It is an age-old debate with many sceptics and many believers. One of the biggest difficulties is separating the religious influence in order to create an objective argument.

Religion Versus Science

In the modern Western world, there would seem to be really only two approaches. The first being the overall Judaic/Islamic/ Christian religious notion that we have one life and at the point of death we have to wait in a state of suspension until 'Judgement Day', before being consigned to heaven or hell, or their equivalents. The second is that we, as human beings, are little more than a cosmic accident of evolution and have no past, no future of any real worth, and we struggle through our days until we die.

The religious debate on life could be perceived as little more than a controlling mechanism. The argument goes as follows: if the established religious hierarchy can persuade people that they will be rewarded in the next life, if only they live a good life in this one, then religious rules on how this can be achieved are a form of control. Many scientists today believe that there are more credible explanations for most of life's great mysteries. Furthermore, it can be said that these so-called mysteries are only mysteries because it would be problematic to both religion *and* materialistic science, if we were able to answer them.

Most stories of ghosts of the past, reincarnation and after death communication – and other communications with those who have passed away – as well as much of the afterlife debate theories, involve religion and its belief in a deity or deities and that there is some type of utopia beyond. Therefore, in order to have an objective (and, personally, much easier) discussion, I think it is best to remove the religious aspect from the debate and aim for a more scientific argument which can offer more tangible proof.

Could There Be an Afterlife?

First, let me start at the very basic level and explore what is meant by the term 'afterlife' – the place where the souls or spirits of the dead (the etheric people) are thought to live on after physical death.

Practically every single society (or significant sections within it) in the world believes in some form or other of the continuing eternal existence of the human spirit or soul, and this belief forms the basis of most religions. To Spiritualists, the truth is that there is no death, just different stages of eternal life that help the soul to progress towards perfection. Other religions subscribe to visions of the world beyond. In Christianity there is heaven – and hell, as an option for the badly behaved, or purgatory as the halfway house. In Islam there is the judgement by Allah, called *akhirah*, whereby the one God decides who goes where. The Buddhist view of the afterlife is that we all reincarnate into different physical bodies until we reach perfection. This belief is termed the samsara cycle and is based on karma. We live here in what is termed the material world, spirits live in the next world in the afterlife and as such they and we are eternal beings.

One of the main problems with life after death is the fact

we are dealing with a frequency, or wavelength, that is beyond our normal senses. (Later, I shall describe how Ronald Pearson discusses this in the context of quantum theory, of wave particle motion, the invisible part of the world.) Our whole world is built on invisible subatomic structures that we cannot see, though all science now accepts and agrees that they exist. If we live by virtue of these invisible structures and energy waves, why do we find it so difficult to comprehend that we leave this dimension vibrating at a certain level, and that our etheric bodies pass naturally into another dimension, also vibrating at a different level which is invisible to us on earth?

The exact location of the afterlife is, up until now, undetermined by science. There has been a hypothesis that uses quantum mechanics (and the newest idea, the 'string theory' of multi-dimensional energy) to explain the existence of another dimension in which spirits live. However, in terms of absolute scientific proof, there has still been no generally accepted concrete evidence. Could it be that there are too many parties with vested interests for there to be just one definitive explanation of the location of the afterlife?

It may happen yet, who knows? Theories like those of Ronald Pearson may become accepted worldwide, but look how many belief and thought structures will have to be changed as a result.

Experiencing the Afterlife

As I discussed in *After Death Communication*, stories, anecdotes and testimonies of visions surrounding the afterlife have appeared in biographies and literature throughout the ages.

However, it wasn't until the end of the 19th century that the subject received proper scientific research. In a study, Marris[1] interviewed widows and found that many spoke of feeling that their husbands were still present; about half of the sample of bereaved people who required psychiatric treatment that Parkes[2] saw, had a similar impression. Again, Rees reported that one in eight widows and widowers had hallucinations (for want of a better word) of hearing their dead spouse speak, and a similar proportion claimed to have seen the deceased. The bereaved who were studied also referred to a general sensation of the presence of the dead person, which could continue for years, and they found it comforted them. Significantly, those who had been happily married reported this the most often.

Ian Stevenson's remarkable paper 'Research into the Evidence of Man's Survival after Death (*Journal of Nervous and Mental Disease*, 185:152, 1977) surveys the history of research into the survival of bodily death and identifies three historical periods that mirror the scientific thinking of their times. At one point, research waned, as many investigators believed that living individuals with 'paranormal' powers were responsible for all the evidence. Now, however, research again proceeds on a broad front, even though hampered by most scientists' outspoken disbelief in the whole business.

The important types of evidence Stevenson reviewed include the speaking of languages not normally known or learned by the subject, OBE, and reincarnation memories – subjects that I am convinced the scientific community would dismiss without examination. However, Stevenson, a professor of psychiatry at the University of Virginia, feels that this contempt is unwarranted, and that most scientists are simply not aware of the vast amount of high-quality data available. His assertion is that the information acquired so far does not actually compel the conclusion that life exists after death but that it certainly infers it strongly.

Sir William Barrett, a Professor of Physics at the Royal College of Science in Dublin, was one of the first to examine the subject seriously. In 1926, he published his findings in a book entitled *Death-bed Visions*. In the many cases he studied, he discovered some interesting aspects of the experience that are not easily explained. It was not uncommon, for example, for the dying people who saw these visions to identify friends and relatives whom they thought were still living. Nevertheless, in each case, according to Barrett, it was later discovered that these people actually were dead. (Remember, conventional communication was not so sophisticated at the time and it might take weeks or even months to learn that a friend or loved one had died.). Barrett found it curious that children quite often expressed surprise that the 'angels' they saw in their dying moments did not have wings. If the death-bed vision is just a simple hallucination – wishful thinking and seeing what one would expect to see – surely a child would see an angel as it is most often depicted in art and literature, that is with large, white wings?

After this, more extensive research into these mysterious visions went on in the 1960s and 1970s, and most notably, in my opinion, by Dr Karlis Osis of the American Society for Psychical Research. In this research, and for a book he published in 1977 entitled *At the Hour of Death*, Osis considered thousands of case studies and interviewed more than 1,000 doctors, nurses and others who attended the dying. The work uncovered a number of fascinating consistencies:

- Although some dying people reported seeing angels and other religious figures (and sometimes even mythical figures), the vast majority claimed to see familiar people who had previously passed away.
- Very often, the friends and relatives seen in these visions expressed directly that they had come to help take them away.
- The dying person was reassured by the experience and expressed great happiness with the vision. (Contrast this with the confusion or fear that a non-dying person would experience at seeing a 'ghost'. The dying also seemed quite willing to go with these apparitions.)
- The dying person's mood – even state of health – seemed to change. During these visions, a once depressed or pain-ridden person was overcome with elation and momentarily relieved of pain until death struck.
- These experiencers did not seem to be hallucinating or to be in an altered state of consciousness, rather they appeared to be quite aware of their real surroundings and conditions.
- Whether or not the dying person believed in an afterlife was irrelevant; the experience and reactions were the same[3].

In the context of experiences at the precise moment of death, and the accompanying experiences of late relatives and past loved ones appearing to lead the dying to the next realm, relatively little systematic work has been done on actual post-mortem visitations to the living[4]. Cleiren's Leiden Study[5] showed that 14 months after a death, about a third of the bereaved people studied felt a sense of presence of the dead and also 'talked' to the dead, either vocally or in a silent inner 'conversation'. Studies suggest that as many as 66 per cent of widows experience apparitions of their departed husbands[6] and, in addition, Finucane's historical analysis of the way in which the ghostly dead appear to the living illustrates the point that, up to the 18th century, ghosts adopted a normal vocal quality, while by the 20th century they tended to be mute[7]. All of this ties in well with the experiences of angels reported to me in a past project. In only one case did a deceased relative speak. However, in some accounts, an angel accompanied the deceased speaking on their behalf, assuring all would be well.

From a time long before the beginning of recorded history, the universal experience of apparitions has found its way into the language and folklore of cultures all over the world. Indeed, the storyline of *Hamlet*, one of Shakespeare's greatest plays, is based around an ADC, as is Dickens' *A Christmas Carol*, where Ebenezer Scrooge's deceased business partner, Jacob Marley, returns to warn him of his fate if he refuses to changes his materialistic values and become more charitable. Although disbelieving at first, Scrooge eventually takes heed of the warning. Then, of course, there are accounts in the Bible, the various appearances Jesus made and visions of the Blessed Virgin Mary are recorded throughout Catholic literature.

An Increasing Belief

Interestingly, one of the most authoritative spokesmen of the Roman Catholic Church recently raised eyebrows among the faithful by declaring that the Church does now, in fact, believe in the feasibility of communication with the dead[8]. The Reverend Gino Concetti, chief theological commentator for the Vatican newspaper *L'Osservatore Romano*, denied he was signalling any change in approach, but agreed that his remarks might come as a surprise to many believers. He said the Church remained opposed to the raising of spirits, but added: 'Communication is possible between those who live on this earth and those who live in

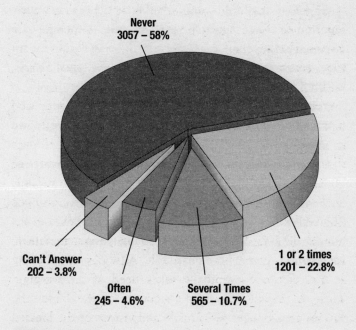

Never
3057 – 58%

Can't Answer
202 – 3.8%

Often
245 – 4.6%

Several Times
565 – 10.7%

1 or 2 times
1201 – 22.8%

Total: 5,270 – 100%

a state of eternal repose, in heaven or purgatory. It may even be that God lets our loved ones send us messages to guide us at certain moments in our life.' He went on to suggest that dead relatives could be responsible for prompting impulses and triggering inspiration – and even for 'sensory manifestations', such as appearances in dreams.

It is also interesting to look at how beliefs are changing. Professor Michael Earl[9], for example, says one might think, amid this socio-cultural evolution, that there would be a decreasing belief in and concern with personal immortality. Like the concerns with demons and witches that used to perturb ancient (and perhaps not so ancient) peoples, we should by now have grown out of this fixation. However, we have not. If anything – and whether it is because we are entering a new spiritual era or not – people are communicating belief in an afterlife and subsequent experiences more and more. Indeed, *General Social Surveys*, NORC[9] have included the question: 'How often have you felt as though you were really in touch with someone who had died?' The data mapped here represents the breakdown of responses:

A massive survey was carried out and has since been updated. Again, this was to assess belief in an afterlife. Surprisingly, in the update to this study, over 39,000 individuals from 32 countries were surveyed. Belief in the afterlife in many countries, the UK included, is definitely increasing.

4

THE PLAUSIBILITY OF ETHER AND AFTERLIFE

'I have been in touch with the minds of certain people who have parted from their bodies. How can a mind get in touch with us when it has no body? It must borrow some material form; but because 'spirits' are discarnate it does not mean they have no bodies. They have substantial bodies, not made up of matter but, as I think, of ether.'

SIR OLIVER LODGE

THERE ARE FEW ARGUMENTS about that try to disprove that there is an afterlife, and there are several reasons for this. Perhaps this is mostly due to the ever-growing number of deity believers out there; and maybe because the people behind the pro-afterlife arguments are more proactive. The main focuses of those who argue that afterlife is simple fallacy is the assertion that human beings naturally enjoy the comfort of believing in life after death (which is where religious belief kicks in) or that humankind has irrational tendencies towards the supernatural.

There is also the claim that NDEs are due to what is termed the 'dying brain condition'. Some even go as far as to credit that belief in an afterlife is instigated to encourage 'good' behaviour – the heaven and hell, or karma idea – similar to the threat of coal from santa in your stocking.

All About Ether

There have been many scientists who have given much of their research time to the quest of finding tangible proof, a mathematical equation or straightforward concrete evidence to prove there is life after death. Indeed, many reputable scientists have believed in the eternal state of being in spite of their more 'scientific' work or fame. Here are some:

- Emmanuel Swedenborg (born in Sweden in 1688) was described as 'an intensely practical man who invented the glider, the submarine and an ear trumpet for the deaf.
- Sir William Crookes discovered the chemical element thallium.
- Thomas Alva Edison, inventor of the phonograph and first electric light bulb was interested in the afterlife and experimented with mechanical means of contacting the 'dead'.
- John Logie Baird, television pioneer and inventor of the infrared camera, contacted the 'deceased' Thomas A. Edison through a medium and later stated: 'I have witnessed some very startling phenomena under circumstances which make trickery out of the question.'
- George Meek was a designer and manufacturer of devices for air conditioning and treatment of waste water but dedicated much time to the study of the afterlife, as did Sigmund Freud and others.

The idea of the existence of ether was conceived before Newton. It was seen as an all-permeating substance which went all throughout the universe, connecting atoms together, connecting all the planets to the sun, and so on. Then Einstein's theory came along, which totally discredited the concept of 'ether', so scientists, in order to avoid discrediting themselves, retreated and returned to saying that ether did not exist.

Nevertheless, ether, I argue, does exist. The structure of it is similar to the network of the human brain, which gives it the potential to be conscious and to grow intellectually. But we are leaping ahead here, and need to examine the developments before revealing the amazing outcome of most recent findings in the last few chapters of this book.

As Sir Oliver Lodge said, the etheric body, the part of us that lives on, is made of this substance known as ether. When the body and brain dies this ether moves to a new dimension.

Of course, 'seeing is believing' is a basic human instinct. We want to test things ourselves rather than rely on another's testimony. A friend of mine sells a special magnet to affix to a pipe in your car, which is said to reduce fuel consumption. When he travels to large haulage firms and trucking corporations, he can offer letters upon letters of thanks from past customers, along with graphs of before and after fuel costs verifying its worth. Yet, still people want to try it for themselves. The proof of the pudding is in the eating. The same is the case for the idea of an afterlife. We can be told it exists. Further, the great religions and belief structures ascertain this. Yet, we still turn to mediums to try and obtain personal proof. While writing this, naturally, I wanted to experience that proof and test it for myself. One of my first experiences was sitting with a clairvoyant and then clairaudient. From that, I progressed to sitting with a trance medium on several occasions. I can still recall how nervous I was – almost sitting on the lap of the person who accompanied me. However, as with most things, the thought seems far worse that the actual deed. As soon as the guides came through, I witnessed transfiguration and found myself speaking, laughing and joking with the etheric people who regularly enter the medium's body amid sessions. However, the evidence, although interesting and immensely philosophical, did not make the phenomenon totally concrete for me. I then visited a direct voice medium. Although becoming more accustomed to the setting and darkened rooms, I was still nervous. Again, I was able to speak to a couple of people in the etheric world, only their voice didn't come from the medium but seemingly from mid-air – I was intrigued. This magical door to another world had now well and truly opened. I have seen enough to know that I am sure there is most definitely something there. But that is my own personal evidence and how could that evidence be explained?

A Lawyer's Case for the Afterlife

I am lucky enough to have communicated with Victor Zammit BA (Psych), MA (Hist), LLB, PhD, a retired solicitor of the Supreme Court of New South Wales and the High Court of Australia. He is also a psychic researcher and lecturer in psychic phenomena. In essence, Victor is a lawyer, a born sceptic as, of course, lawyers have to be. With his interests and background, he wanted to see if there was legal proof, sufficient to convince a learned judge and a jury of 12 sound and true people that: 'There is without any doubt whatsoever scientific evidence for the existence of the afterlife.'

In his book *A Lawyer Presents the Case for the Afterlife: The Irrefutable, Objective Evidence*[1], Zammit presents 23 different areas of evidence showing that the existence of the afterlife can be proved 'absolutely' – evidence which he believes would be accepted by the highest court in any civilised country. He says:

'...there is undeniable scientific evidence today for the afterlife. I am an open-minded sceptic lawyer, a former practising attorney-at-law formally qualified in a number of university disciplines. The argument that follows is not just an abstract, theoretical, academic legal argument. As an open minded investigator I set out to investigate the existing evidence for survival and with others to create conditions to test for ourselves claims that communication with intelligences from the afterlife is possible'.

His investigations into the existence of an afterlife included many arguments from esteemed and respected scientists. His arguments are based on experimentation and the results obtained from the use of cerebral techniques: electronic voice phenomena (EVP), which involve tape recordings which pick up spirit voices that the human ear cannot; instrumental transcommunication (ITC), which is contact with the dead via radio, over telephones, on television, on answering machines and on faxes and computers; psychic laboratory experiments; cross-correspondences; and proxy sittings. In addition, in relation to the issue of materialisation, he discusses Einstein's famous formula $E = mc^2$; and also explores the Scole experiments, trans and mental mediumship, poltergeists, xenoglossy, reincarnation, NDE, OBE, afterlife intelligence examples and other afterlife investigations[2]. An impressive range, one must admit.

Zammit states that he does not reject any evidence just because the evidence is not consistent with our own beliefs, saying that we tend to be products of our own environment, our own upbringing. From the time we are born, we absorb information from our family, friends, schools, and the media. Also, we must not forget that we are born into a world environment with its own unique culture, history and tradition. Inevitably, beliefs become deeply emotional; they are also neurological. We know that when we hear any information not consistent with our own cherished beliefs, we tend to reject that information. Why? Our mind will put up defences to protect our bias, our partiality, because inconsistent information will give us anxiety, elicit fear and will tend to destabilise us emotionally. For example, many Christians, of whatever church, persuasion or sect can become very disturbed when told that their view of things is 'wrong'. Similarly, if you were born in the Middle East, you are very likely to be a Moslem and, in some instances, you would have recited *Allah Akbah* ('God is Great') a number of times already, and it will have become a strongly engrained belief. Equally, if you were born in India, China or Japan you would have totally different world view and beliefs to a Westerner.

Whenever there is an inconsistency between 'scientific' knowledge and traditional or 'personal beliefs', inevitably scientific knowledge prevails over personal beliefs. It cannot be any other way. Remember what happened in Italy at the time of scientist Galileo, who used his knowledge of science and stated that the earth is not in the centre of the universe and that it is the earth that revolves around the Sun – not the other, accepted, way around. It was a view deemed to be heretical. Nevertheless, eventually, after many years, the Christian Catholic Church had to accept that science prevailed over religious beliefs and admitted it was wrong. It is also an excellent example of the continuous refinement in human knowledge.

This is a critical piece of information. Ultimately, what is important for you to know and fully understand on this planet is *only the truth based on information that can be repeatedly tested for validity*.

The evidence Dr Zammit corroborated was been sent to experts around the world – to theologians, to scientists, to materialists and hardcore sceptics – for evaluation and fault-finding. Ten years later, no scientist – no biologist, no physicist, no sceptical empiricist, no materialist – no one – has been able to rebut the evidence for the existence of the afterlife. On his website, his sponsors are offering the sum of US $1,000,000 for anyone anywhere who can demonstrate that the evidence for the afterlife, as published in his research on the internet, is not correct. It still remains unclaimed and Dr Zammit states:

'After many years of serious investigation I have come to the irretrievable conclusion that there is a great body of evidence which taken as a whole absolutely and unqualifiedly proves the case for the afterlife. I will not be arguing that the objective evidence has just very high value. Nor am I suggesting that this evidence be accepted beyond reasonable doubt. I am arguing that the evidence taken as a whole constitutes overwhelming and irrefutable proof for the existence of the afterlife. There have been millions of pages written about "psychic" phenomena and scientific research into the afterlife. Using my professional background as an attorney and my university training in psychology, history and scientific method, I have very carefully selected aspects of "psychic" research and afterlife knowledge which would technically constitute objective evidence in the Supreme Court of the United States, the House of Lords in England, the High Court of Australia and in every civilised legal jurisdiction around the world.'

It may seem odd to those of us brought up in a Western, or supposedly Christian setting, but we doubting nations are in a minority in the wider world. Roughly three-quarters of the world's population have religions that fully accept an afterlife, of a kind, and it is part of their culture. It is surely an irony, I feel, that the Christian culture is the most recalcitrant to accept the evidence that we all survive physical death. After all, it is the very religion in which Jesus is said to have risen from death – with witnesses! Yet, not too many within its widest folds challenge the doctrine and it is only characters like David Jenkins, the former Bishop of Durham,[3] who are controversial enough to speak out on the matter.

In conclusion, then, I think the biggest argument that I can offer you in favour of there being an afterlife is that no scientist has yet proved that the afterlife does *not* exist.

5

THE PART OF US
THAT LIVES ON

'One man's truth is another man's prejudice.'

ANON

EVEN SUCH APPARENTLY disparate fields of investigation as religion and science share a common motive
– the pursuit of truth. Our quest for the truth has been
analogised, with various nations and cultures making an
ascent of the same mountain from different sides. This
analogy could be extended to include all the assorted skills
of engineering, physics, chemistry and mathematics on the
one side, and the arts, literature, painting, sculpture, drama,
music and dance on the other. They are all an examination,
exposition, expression and explanation of multitudinous
aspects of the human condition, each and all trying to
reconcile the limits of human nature and our physical
environment with our urge to achieve our highest ideals and
aspirations. The word 'science' derives from the Latin
scientia, meaning 'knowledge' or 'to know'.

Current thought seems to exalt the worldly and material at the expense of the spiritual, which has rather fallen into disrepute and only seems to receive scant attention and regard. People only seem to want to accept things as being true if they can be replicated again and again under strict laboratory conditions. For example, it seems that phenomena such as physical mediumship will only be taken seriously when infrared cameras are publicly allowed to record the events and the results are widely seen by the general public.

Will we ever be able to convince people that there does seem to be some other reality aside from the one that we all live and breath? Will they accept this same plane of being, with which some gifted people are able to communicate? Will others be believed who have connected to it via meditation or having had an OBE or NDE? Or those those who have had a communication with it through the use of drugs, channelling, pendulums, visiting a medium or clairvoyant, or by having had some sort of spiritual or religious experience to mention but a few ways?

When Crookes published the results of his revolutionary experiments in 1874, it simply provided a rational scientific explanation for the mountain of evidence that existed for thousands of years. Since these experiments have been repeated with contemporary, fully developed, materialisation mediums (such as Helen Duncan and Rita Lorraine), an awful lot of questions have been answered. In a nutshell, materialisation and the scientific evidence behind it now seems to connect everything together. We will never have all the answers, but a major step forward in scientific endeavour has taken place. It is as Jung believed:

that just as the human embryo develops through the stages of evolutionary history, so the mind also travels on its on evolutionary journey.

The Mind and Brain Debate

Specifically, though, what of that part of us which seems to live on? What is the bit of us – mind, consciousness, soul, spirit or personality – that ends up on the ceiling during a NDE?

If one were to follow Einstein's model of the universe, the case for the mind dying with the brain is concrete. Parapsychologists and orthodox scientific teaching have promulgated this time and time again across all disciplines, from philosophy through to physics. However, I believe sincerely that the mind and brain are separate; and I consider that my assertion is now accompanied by overwhelming scientific proof. This is a conclusion that I am sure can be drawn from Ronald Pearson's theory, and through research from other experts in the field such as Peter Wadhams, for it all follows logically from Christiaan Huygen's and Sir Oliver Lodge's theory about the ether and extends Sir Isaac Newton's model of the universe to match up with recent discoveries in subatomic and quantum physics.

What is Consciousness?

The amount of material written about human consciousness is huge, and by its sheer profusion would have one believe we understood the subject well. However, there are some facts that need to be considered:

- Consciousness has never been observed.
- Consciousness has never been weighed or measured.
- The source of consciousness is unknown.

Its location, within or without the body, despite many trials, has never been discovered.

No one has determined what consciousness consists of, or what it contains. There is not a single scientific proof that consciousness is biological. Therefore, it appears that all the material written about consciousness remains largely subjective.

In his book *The Emperor's New Mind*, Roger Penrose, eminent physicist and winner of the prestigious Wolf Prize, states simply: 'We don't have a good definition of consciousness because we don't know what it is.' So, taking this stand, we really do not know what it is: only that it exists. In other words, consciousness remains undefined and so the only way in which I can define it here is by talking about the mind – the life force – that which separates from the brain when the physical body ceases to live. It is *this* life force (or 'consciousness') that then continues to operate in the normally invisible part of the universe. Of course, such an idea is not new. Alexander Graham Bell', the inventor of the telephone, was actually urged by his family to seek psychiatric evaluation, as they could not understand his insistence and belief that the human voice could be sent great distances through a wire. Along the same lines, in its early days, people may well have believed the television receiver was the actual source of the images and sounds it presented, that is that the images/sounds were stored somewhere within the television set itself, with different items being shown when the position of the channel knob was adjusted. They may even have removed the cover to look for them, trying to discover how the thing worked. One 'expert' actually accused Logie Baird of hiding a midget in his TV set! Yet, for some, it seems that any crazy explanation will do, and in exactly the same way, it need not even be the right one that has the potential to upset the religious and scientific apple cart. However, no matter how much they examined the television receiver, they would not have found the images and sounds stored within.

Science has a similar problem with the human brain. Your body is a 'tool of communication' for your consciousness (the real you) to use while exploring the physical realm. No matter how hard or long scientists examine the brain for things like consciousness, memory, mind, personality, dreams, NDE, OBE, and so on, they will not be found. It seems that the brain is not the source of these events. There is no proof that the NDE – or any other event, for that matter – originates *within* the brain. Nothing has been found stored there. Stimulating the brain at different points in order to produce different reactions and feelings does not actually prove any of them are filed within the brain – just as adjusting the channels on a TV set doesn't prove the images/sounds produced can be found within it.

If, in a post-mortem, someone were to cut open the head of a dead person, the brain would still be there. It is the life force behind it, the mind, that drove this organ, which has gone. Anyone who has seen a dead body will agree that it is literally lifeless. It doesn't look asleep; it looks like a mere shell. It feels as though the 'person' has left it, in spite of the fact that the body with its face and clothes are there before you.

Albert Einstein was one of the most intelligent and prolific contributors to science in the 20th century. His brain was donated to science for studies of how he acquired such great intelligence. Yet, researchers found that Einstein's brain was smaller than most, and contained nothing unusual. It did, however, possess a larger number of synapses, the minute space between one nerve cell and another nerve cell, through which nerve impulses are transmitted from one to the other. He had more 'connections' than the average person, more 'channels' for his consciousness to use. The more you use your brain, the more synapses develop.

Scientists are looking for a biologically-based trigger to explain the NDE and other consciousness events. They often say, 'We know it is there, we just haven't found it yet.' However, the truth is – they don't know it's there. Obviously, in order to know it's there, it would need to be found. So, without any biological evidence whatsoever, some scientists continue to declare publicly that NDE are biological. I consider this to be extremely unfair to the experiencers, characterising them as witless, simultaneously passing misinformation about NDE to the general public.

The search for a biological basis of consciousness has been going on for more than a hundred years, without any significant results. How many more years will pass before science realises the brain is not the source of consciousness and that this consciousness (or mind, spirit or soul) is something separate?

Put Up – or Shut Up!

As stated above, I believe there is proof – and that it is as conclusive as proof can get – clear, solid proof that we are spiritual 'beings' inhabiting a physical body. In the future, I hope that scientists and others concerned with NDE will consider the preponderance of evidence before telling the general public or experiencers that NDE cases are just biological events. Then we can all benefit from this 'knowledge of self' and learn to grow spiritually. Yet before this, the current sceptics will need to show proof of two things.

First, they need to prove there is tangible, biological evidence of consciousness, memory, NDE, and so on, existing within the physical brain; and that this evidence can be collaborated by their peers. Second, they need to prove how this biological consciousness can remain alive and capable of gathering information on the body's surroundings while the body is in a state of clinical death – when it is showing no brain, heart or respiratory response of any kind – in order to promote their theory that humankind is wholly biological and has no future beyond death.

So, in the name of truth, I feel that it is time for sceptics to present their biological proof. On the other hand, until they do, they should cease calling NDE some sort of biological misfire.

6

LOOSE ENDS: TYING IT ALL TOGETHER

'The most beautiful thing we can experience is the mysterious.
It is the source of all true art and science.
He to whom the emotion is a stranger, to whom no longer
pause to wonder and stand rapt in awe, is as good as dead.
If his mind and eyes are closed.'

ALBERT EINSTEIN

IF OUR TRUE BEING LIVES on and becomes a separate entity from our brain when that dies, we can make sense of a lot of other phenomena. This seems the point in an ongoing examination, at which we might pull together a few, seemingly, disparate elements.

Xenoglossy
Xenoglossy is the ability of a person to speak or write a foreign language, which they never knew, learnt or spoke before. After all other possible explanations – such as fraud, genetic memory, telepathy and cryptomnesia (latent or subconscious memory) – have been investigated, xenoglossy is often taken as evidence of memories of a language learned in a past life. (Of course, this explanation

is somewhat problematic and is one I discuss below). A more likely explanation in my opinion is that xenoglossy is communication with a discarnate entity – an etheric person (think of the film *Stigmata*). Considerable proof of the latter was provided by a lady named Rose, who came to England from Holland in order to witness one of the Rita Lorraine experiments. Her 'dead' son, who was killed in the army, and her mother, both fully materialised; and the three of them spoke together in fluent Dutch. At the time of writing, a taped copy of her story is being translated into English to add to the evidence[1].

As we saw in Chapter 2, the Brazilian physical medium Mirabelli had only a basic education and spoke only his native language. Yet, when he was in trance, spirit beings spoke through him in 26 different languages, including German, French, Dutch, four Italian dialects, Czech, Arabic, Japanese, Spanish, Russian, Turkish, Hebrew, Albanian, several African dialects, Latin, Chinese, modern Greek, Polish, Syrio-Egyptian and ancient Greek. Also while he was in trance, high-level spirits delivered through him verbal presentations on difficult subjects far beyond his own understanding; such talks included topics like medicine, jurisprudence, sociology, political economy, politics, theology, psychology, history, the natural sciences, astronomy, philosophy, logic, music, spiritism, occultism and literature[2].

While in trance, Mirabelli also exhibited the faculty of automatic writing in 28 different languages, writing at a speed that normal penmanship cannot reach. In a mere quarter hour he wrote out some five pages in Polish on 'The Resurrection of Poland'; in 20 minutes he wrote nine pages in Czech on 'The Independence of Czechoslovakia'; in 12 minutes he set down four pages in Hebrew on 'Slander'; in 40 minutes, 25 pages in Persian on 'The Instability of Great Empires'; in 15 minutes, four pages of Latin on 'Famous Translations'; in 12 minutes, five pages in Japanese on 'The Russian-Japanese War'; in 22 minutes, 15 pages in Syrian on 'Allah and his Prophets'; in 15 minutes, eight pages of Chinese on 'An Apology for Buddha'; in 15 minutes, eight pages in Syrio-Egyptian on 'The Fundamentals of Legislation'; and in 32 minutes, three pages of hieroglyphics which have not yet been deciphered[3].

The same sort of thing has since been displayed by Alec Harris and countless other mediums and psychic people today. I am convinced that it can all be taken as 'evidence' for an afterlife.

Dis-ease: Ourselves and Our Spacesuits

At present, each of us is in a physical body, our shell or our 'spacesuit', which equips us for life on earth. Quite simply, if we abuse or mistreat our body, it goes wrong. If we look after it, it sees us through without any major glitches.

It is becoming accepted commonly, not just in Jungian psychology, that as we develop through childhood, teens and into adulthood, aspects of our character emerge – things which we really can't abide or issues which we have tried to block out. When they come to light, it's our natural reaction to push them back down into the darkness of unconsciousness – to disown them or pretend they don't exist. It is very much as Oscar Wilde put it: 'Only the shallow fully understand themselves'. Or, expressed in psychological language, this process is described as 'repression'. We repress the things we do not like in ourselves – ways of behaving, thoughts and attitudes to other people and of ourselves, thoughts and impulses which we consider dirty or disgusting, things that make us scared or afraid, and so forth. It is our way of trying to get rid of them – brushing them under the carpet. But it doesn't work – or, rather, it works only for a while. As Jung said: 'What we repress in ourselves disappears from within but reappears in our environment.' In other words, the naughty or nasty psychological energies come back in other forms – for example, in the way other people deal with us, or as diseases we contract later on in life.

Science is advancing so much and so fast that it is being accepted more and more that a number of illness or diseases are created by us from such feelings and emotions which have not been dealt with. But it is these emotions and life lessons that enable us to grow and help us on our way – we are all, in essence, on a spiritual quest. We could even go so far as to say that we are simply spiritual beings having a physical experience. This notion that organic diseases and some illnesses are a simple outward expression of the state of the mind at the time, or of built up repressed feelings coming from the personality rather than simply arising in the body, can be highlighted by looking at cases of schizophrenia and multiple personality, where the human body behaves differently according to the 'personality' that is occupying it. For example, there are instances of a person being diabetic when one personality is present, but not diabetic when another is present. I canot help but feel that this, surely, points to at least some forms of diabetes originating from thoughts and not simply in the physical body? Of course, this idea would horrify most people as it runs completely counter to conventional understanding, which places the body first and treats thoughts as a kind of 'add-on' to the physical.

As another example, the summer of 2003, when I was undertaking the most serious research for this book – was the first time that I had ever experienced *real* stress and anxiety. For the two years prior to the really serious investigations, an awful lot had happened, most of which I laughed off and brushed under the carpet. I never dealt with it. Then came writing this book. Unlike previous 'nine-to-five' projects, this one involved much internal research and questioning; for once I had to focus on me – my life – not someone else's. Death enveloped me, I couldn't switch off from it and I spent *all* day thinking. The stress of that alone came out in the form of intense anxiety. On the surface, I had everything I could ever ask for. I thought I was immensely happy, until, seemingly out of nowhere, I began to suffer terrifying panic attacks, feelings of unreality and disorientation took over. I lost all sense of who I was and what I was. It was as if I was in limbo and couldn't get back onto the correct path. For the first time ever I felt alone and afraid, as if I was trapped in my own skin yet detached & different. My research findings were breaking down my beliefs – I was losing all structure & comprehension. My reaction was to climb into my cave and try and make sense and work through it all – very quickly I had become the complete opposite from my normal self and it terrified me – which, of course, added to the angst.

It was only when I fell completely apart, momentarily incapable of doing anything and feeling the most alone I have ever felt, that I finally asked for help. It was then, mercifully, that the floodgates opened and everything from the past 2 years came pouring out. All of those unpleasant feelings were simply an outward manifestation of the scramble and torment going on in my mind at the time – this book was the icing on the cake which tipped the balance – being ill was my body's way of pulling on the brakes and saying, 'Stop and sort all this out before you do anything else.' As Jung said, 'A person's symptoms will often make perfect sense in light of their own individual story. The problem is always the whole person, never the symptom alone and so often this is ignored.'

Emotional pain and internal conflict is so hard for others to handle. I recall some years ago that the mental health charity and campaign MIND ran a poster showing a beautiful healthy girl saying: 'I have forgotten my nervous breakdown, but my friends haven't.' A sad, but true reflection of our societies attitude to nervous and mental illness – even though, as I know myself – one can emerge at the other side probably far more stable than ever before.

This 'stiff upper lip' attitude is why people try and keep things in and cope. As a young child, if we fall over and graze our knee, we can be guaranteed a hug and the injury washed and covered with a sticking plaster. However, a child who said he was scared or sad may well get the reply: 'Afraid? Don't be silly. Big boys of ten shouldn't be afraid!' or 'What have you got to be sad about? We're going to Florida in the summer⁵!' Emotional pain, no matter what our age, is all a bit embarrassing really – and of course, not very British. Is it any wonder, I ask myself, that the psychiatric departments are full to the brim?

This notion of our mind being a precursor for physical illness is another way of saying that if illness and disease are not physiological, then the root cause comes from the real 'us', that is, from internal conflicts. In other words, the person we are now and the person we eternally remain is all well and good, but to the shallow can present a problem.

The danger is that someone could say to a person with a disease: 'You can cure yourself by simply thinking about yourself in a different manner.' That really isn't on, for how would *you* feel if someone were blithely to say to you to: 'You can get rid of your cancer; just think differently about yourself and you'll be cured' or 'Pull yourself together – all these irrational things are all in your head!' If only it were easy to do this. For many people, the thoughts and feelings are deeply embedded, having formed over years. It is not a case of just *thinking* differently. In some cases, such as anxiety and depression, a person sometimes needs to get to that level so that they have a giant clean up of the unconscious. In order to allow the floodgates to open, the person needs to loose their armour and become so weak so that they can't hold back the pain any longer. The tremendous energy involved in the long-term suppression of feelings is discharged, leaving the person tired, but in a state where it is finally possible to heal[6].

So, while it may be true that diseases originate in the personality, the cures, depending on the strength of the disease, must involve much more than simply 'thinking differently'. However, in the case of the sceptics, what does such an assertion imply? Does it mean, for example, that every common cold we get is somehow down to what we believe or think, or a culmination of repressed feelings?

Most would reject that, saying that colds are caused by bugs 'doing the rounds'. On the other hand, when there are bugs going round, some people get sick and others do not. Then again, some sickness is viral and/or contagious. So, perhaps those illnesses that break out in our bodies and are not contagious work differently? Are these things decided by the inner mind of the person, albeit subconscious? Whatever the cause, it does seem unlikely that a way could be found to determine whether or not this was the case? For example, tests might reveal that there is a statistical correlation between eating large amounts of tomato ketchup and suffering a brain tumour, or large amounts of butter and having a heart attack. Nevertheless, the fact is that there are also people who eat large amounts of ketchup or butter and never have a brain tumour or heart attack, but this is rarely noted. Modern society would have us believe that eating the 'wrong' foods will cause illness. But is this strictly true? You see, again, we have all heard of people who, although they have adhered to a healthy diet, have died young.

When you think about all these things, it would seem that you are constrained to consider them in terms of the individual – and that implies these are spiritual matters. Jung said that he could never understand why other doctors were so obsessed with making firm diagnoses and not being in the least interested in what their patients had to *say*.

So, then, it does seem plausible that problems, like diseases, can and do occur at the spiritual level. Further, we must go on to say that any 'cure' of the disease has got to come, not from mere changes in thinking, but from spiritual changes and mindsets in the person. Remember, above all, that spiritual changes are deep things, achieved only with considerable effort. As Buddha said: 'All that we are is the result of what we have thought; it is founded on our thoughts, it is made up of our thoughts. If a man speaks or acts with a pure thought, happiness follows him like a shadow that never leaves him.'

Amputees and Phantom Limbs

Losing a small part of our spacesuit doesn't mean we lose a bit of our etheric body. In this form of thinking, when a person loses a limb, it is only the 'physical' body that is damaged – the spacesuit that we use during our short stay on planet earth. The etheric body – that layer that surrounds us, the body we use when we dream, have an NDE or OBE – remains perfect. However, for recognition purposes, etheric people are able to return with their limb missing. It is this etheric body that can re-materialise when people witness an ADC or can be induced in a physical sitting. This theory fits in with what the materialised have said. For example, amid one sitting, Russell Byrne said: 'We can alter our etheric bodies. I am coming back as the nine-year-old boy my parents lost, but I can make myself older when I want to.' Remember that Gwen Byrne, his mother, has also seen a materialised Russell as a fully-grown, young man.

There is a traditional, magical belief that a separated part of the body still retains a connection with the whole by a kind of 'action at a distance', or non-local connection. Rupert Sheldrake reminisces how he first encountered this way of thinking when living in Malaysia[7]. One day, while staying in a *kampong* (Malay village), he was cutting his fingernails, throwing the parings into a nearby bush. When his hosts saw this, they were horrified, explaining that his enemy might pick them up and use them to harm him by witchcraft. They were amazed that he did not know that bad things done to his nail clippings could cause bad things to happen to him. Of course, this connects to voodoo and related practices and beliefs.

Such beliefs are very widespread, and are one of the fundamental principles of sympathetic magic, expressed concisely by the anthropologist James Frazer: 'Things which have once been in contact with each other continue to act on each other at a distance after the physical contact has been severed.'

One of the most intriguing features of quantum theory is that the principle of non-locality – as expressed in the Einstein-Podolsky-Rosen paradox and Bell's Theorem makes much the same point about physical processes in the subatomic realm[8].

In relation to phantom limbs, the belief is that the fate of the severed limb continues to affect the person of whom it was once part. Stories received from readers of *Veterans of Foreign Wars* magazine show that this tradition is alive and well.

When people lose a flesh-and-blood limb, they do not usually lose the *sense* of its presence. It feels as if it is really there, even though it is no longer materially real. What kind of reality does the phantom have? In addition to a sense of its shape, position, and movement, amputees generally experience various feelings within the missing limb, such as itching, warmth, and twisting. Phantom limbs can generally be moved at will, and they also move in coordination with the rest of the body. Indeed, they are felt to be part of the body.

People who wear artificial limbs usually take them off to go to bed, and then the phantom may become very painful. William Warner, an American veteran who lost his right leg above the knee in Italy in 1944, described this experience as follows: 'I get it so bad at times I am unable to sleep. I have talked to a few doctors, but there isn't much they can do. Sometimes at night I get up and put my limb on and walk around, it helps some. As soon as I take it off, it starts in again.'

Oliver Sacks has described a similar case where the amputee explicitly thought of the phantom in two different ways: the good phantom that animated his prosthesis and allowed him to walk, and the bad phantom that hurt when the prosthesis was off at night. Sacks comments: 'With this patient, with all patients, is not use all-important, in dispelling a 'bad' (or passive, or pathological) phantom, if it exists, and in keeping the 'good' phantom alive, active, and well?'

A famous case is in circulation about a man who had a finger amputated and preserved in a jar. The man was OK for several years. Then he went back to his doctor, who had amputated his finger, complaining of a feeling of extreme cold and pain in the missing finger. The doctor wanted to know where the jar with the missing finger was. The man told him it was in his mother's heated basement, where it had always been. The doctor told the man to call his mother and check the jar. The mother reluctantly when to check and found a broken basement window a few inches from the jar. As soon as the finger was warmed up the pain left the man.

Out-of-Body Experiences (OBE)

Continuing from phantom limbs, we enter the closely related phenomena of out-of-the-body experiences. In an OBE, people find themselves 'outside' their bodies, implicitly or explicitly within a kind of phantom body.

The OBE occurs when a person's duplicate invisible body – sometimes called the astral body or etheric body – is able to move outside of their physical body with full consciousness. For most people there is no control at all over the OBE; it just happens. Furthermore, a person who experiences an OBE does not have to be ill or near death. Indeed, those who have had an OBE usually accept that they survive physical death. They know that the reason why they return to their physical body is because their invisible duplicate body is still connected to the physical body by a silver cord. When the silver cord is irretrievably severed, the invisible body (to the physical eye) continues to survive in the afterworld. The OBE is an historical occurrence and has been reported from all around the world for over 20 centuries.

Dutch scientists succeeded in weighing the physical body before, during and after exteriorisation (OBE). They found a weight loss of 2¼ ounces during exteriorisation[9]. Professor Kimberly Clark of the University of Washington reported a case, now internationally known, in which a woman hospital patient who was suffering from cardiac arrest had an OBE. Her duplicate, invisible body went for an astral journey on the higher floors of the hospital. She ended up in a storeroom she had obviously never been into before and here she saw an old tennis shoe on top of the lockers. On returning to her body and coming into consciousness, she related the experience to the professor. Stunned by this information, the professor set out to check her story. Everything to the very last detail was confirmed – even the tennis shoe's manufacturer.

All of us have similar experiences in our dreams, when we seem to travel far and wide – some even experience premonitions of future events – even though our physical body remains in the same place throughout, fast asleep in bed. Some people have dreams in which they know that they are dreaming, known as 'lucid dreams'. They still have a dream body, but now they can will where they go, and to some extent control their experience. Such dreams are very like OBE, the main difference being that one is entered from the dreaming state, one from the waking. In esoteric literature, travelling in lucid dreams, or in out-of-the-body experiences, is known as 'astral travel', and the body in which this happens is usually referred to as the 'astral body', 'non-material body' or 'subtle body'. (Again, we have the problem of language – for I believe this body to be the same as the etheric body – the part of us that lives on.)

Such experiences have been known in most, if not all, traditional cultures. Even in modern industrial societies, they are far from uncommon. Surveys have repeatedly shown that between 10 and 20 percent of the population remember having at least one OBE.

Near Death Experiences (NDE)

The OBE element is the beginning of a NDE, whereby experiencers find themselves free from, and outside their body. They feel as though they are still alive – which they are. They can still see and hear the surrounding activity.

They feel different, but are still basically the same person outside their body as they were inside it. The NDE element only begins the moment the body stops. It is at this point that 'something' leaves the body — and it is this 'something' that, in NDE circles, is often referred to as the 'individual vitality' of the experiencer. Apparently, it is usually very surprised to find itself free of the body and still alive. It is this 'vitality' or spirit, soul, personality, consciousness, essence, astral or etheric body which lives on.

NDE survivors talk of 'light tunnels', 'life reviews', 'feeling surrounded by love'; speaking with 'deceased friends', 'light beings', and many have verbalised 'the light' as being 'God', or some such equivalent from other culturally centred beliefs. They speak of knowing that they were in the presence of 'higher intelligence' — an intelligence that loved and cared for them. Not many wanted to return to their body, as this place was more desirable. Nevertheless, return they did — for one reason or another.

It seems that people take more from NDE than any other; they bring back an expanded perception of what life is about and they leave behind any fear of death. This is a little different for every person who has an NDE. These events have been catalogued, compared and analysed in many ways. But, the only way that matters is the personal meaning the NDE has to the experiencer. It is this meaning, that almost always causes profound personality and lifestyle changes in the experiencer. Some leave their current jobs and re-train in the caring professions. Others undertake volunteer work at hospices, nursing homes and hospitals. Some begin classes or support groups for other survivors. Even those who don't 'go public' with their experience are 'changed' into kinder, more loving individuals. Put simply: the impact of the experience is 'to change the experiencer' and the 'change' lasts a lifetime. There are hundreds of NDE/OBE accounts in print, and estimates range from thousands to millions of NDE/OBE occurrences that have not been published.

Scientists are divided regarding OBE/NDE – some accept and some reject. The main argument against is centred on brain chemistry. There are many published accounts of how brain activity can produce 'thoughts, visions, and hallucinations' that are similar in content to the NDE. This may well be correct, but the experiencer would be unaware of these since he or she is out-of-body at this time – and thoroughly enjoying the new view of the surroundings. Let us take an analogy; asthma-like symptoms can be induced through the inhalation of carbon dioxide, but this is not *causing* asthma. All that it is doing is creating the same effects. It is not spontaneous and not necessarily the same experience as someone having a one-off spontaneous attack. So it may be the same with any brain-chemistry explanation of NDE.

Much has been published on NDE, especially by Melvin Morse, a paediatrician and neuroscientist who has written many books on the subject of young children and their NDEs. The validation for his study is that the children are often so young, they have not yet 'absorbed our adult views and ideas of death'. Morse has interviewed hundreds of children, and received many of the same positive responses of an afterlife and out-of-body experiences. However, on the other side of the coin, there is Susan Blackmore's research. She explains NDE as being a result of lack of oxygen to the brain – so that when we die we die, and that is it! She believes that an afterlife is nothing more than an idea fabricated for our own comfort. She explains:

'All things considered, I can see no reason to adopt the afterlife hypothesis. I am sure I shall remain in a minority for a long time to come, especially among NDE but for me the evidence and the arguments are overwhelming. We are biological organisms, evolved in fascinating ways for no purpose at all and with no end in mind. We are simply here and this is how it is. I have no self and "I" own nothing. There is no one to die. There is just this moment, and now this, and now this[10].'

To me, this is a scant, blinkered and narrow view of the phenomenon, but there are various reasons why such arguments are put forward, be it a suppression of knowledge or whatever. The poet T.S Eliot remarked that 'man cannot stand a meaningless existence', but I don't think that means we have to invent a meaning.

For some time, the general consensus has been to tell the general public or experiencers that NDE and OBE are merely biological events. Yet, I believe strongly that, like angel visions, ADC – and now – materialisation phenomena, we do have a right to know what is going on, and not merely have things explained away for the sake of it. This especially is the case so if these are real occurrences and can help us develop and understand ourselves, and, of course, learn to grow more spiritually. I have never read of hallucinations, delusions, or any other kind of misperception that produced such positive changes in large numbers of scattered individuals. What these individuals experienced certainly had to be real.

I am convinced that as far as spontaneous, non-induced experiences (in other words *not* including mediums and psychics as part of this argument) are concerned, OBE/NDE and such are as conclusive as proof gets. What the arguments and scientific findings regarding consciousness, OBE and NDE provide us with seem to be solid proof that humans are indeed spiritual 'beings', simply inhabiting a physical body. The evidence is already here, but our scientific knowledge is not yet sufficient to reproduce it or demonstrate it. But then we can't reproduce "love", yet we know it exists …? It goes back to the human need of seeing is believing.

Medical experience of NDE

There have been enormous advances in medicine over the past few decades, with advances in resuscitation techniques making it ever more possible to revive patients who have died on the operating table. One of the unexpected effects of such advances is that many patients, who have died and been revived, go on to report experiences they had during the period of their operation. Such experiences have proved fascinating, and a whole field of research into these so-called NDE has grown, with an increasing number of people conducting investigations of a scientific nature into them.

However, if a patient who has died during an operation and been revived then reports that he met his late grandmother during this period, a sceptic might well ask whether the experience of meeting with his grandmother occurred at the precisely the same time that the patient was dead on the operating table. Perhaps, the operation had been one-hour long, during which the patient was clinically dead for 5 minutes. In such an event, the investigation would have to be sure that the patient's experience of meeting with his grandmother occurred *within* the specific 5 minutes that he was dead, and not at some other time during the remaining 55 minutes.

One needs to be sure that the phenomena being studied are what they are claimed to be – in this case, experiences had after dying. In this case, the investigation needs to eliminate, for example, the possibility that the patient was not properly anaesthetised and had had a hallucination during the time of the operation but not at the time he was dead.

One case, which definitely defeats the sceptics, occurred at the Barrow Institute for Neurological Research in Phoenix, Arizona. There, a daring surgeon was performing a new procedure on a lady called Pam Reynolds. Because of the nature of the operation, both her body and brain had to be brought to a complete standstill, so she was clinically dead throughout the entire procedure. The paragraph below is a description of the event in Leroy Kattein's NDE newsgroup (reproduced with kind permission):

'She [Pam Reynolds] was having surgery performed to remove an aneurism from her brain. Her body was cooled to below 60 degrees F and all of the blood was drained from her brain. Her ECG and brain stem response showed no activity, the definition of brain death in many states. During all of this, she reported rising from her body and seeing the operation performed below her. She also reported contact with 'The Light' and many of her deceased relatives. Remember, she had no brain activity whatsoever. Even hallucinations register brain activity. It is interesting that upon recovering she recounted accurately many details of her operation, including conversations heard and a description of the surgical instruments. It has been postulated by a NDE sceptic, that Pam overheard the sounds in the room and generated a 'mental map' of things around her. However, what the sceptic failed to acknowledge is that instruments were inserted into Pam's ears that generated clicks to measure brain stem response. Her brain stem response throughout the surgery was inactive. If conversations were heard, her brain stem response should have registered them.'

Pam said:

'I remember seeing several things in the operating room when I was looking down. It was the most aware that I think that I have ever been in my entire life ... I was metaphorically sitting on [the doctor's] shoulder. It was not like normal vision. It was brighter and more focused and clearer than normal vision...'

Now, according to Pam, she was present, above her body, viewing the whole surgical operation, with her consciousness, memory, personality – her whole individuality – intact. She proved this with an accurate, detailed description of the instruments, conversation, and procedures used during the surgery. At the same time, science – using scientific monitoring instruments – was proving that her body was dead. No brain response, no heart response, no response of any kind. The blood had been drained from her body, and the operation lasted for approximately two hours.

This shows clearly that, although her body was dead, Pam was still there somewhere around the operating theatre. This is demonstrated by several items in her report of what happened. For example, she saw and subsequently described the bone saw that the surgeon was using – an instrument that she is unlikely ever to have seen before – as looking like an electric toothbrush. A doctor investigating her report, said it didn't seem very likely that this instrument would look like an electric toothbrush – that is, until he checked out what bone saws look like and found that her description was accurate. Even more amazing is that in addition to her observation of the bone saw, Pam Reynolds also related a conversation between the theatre staff – a conversation that was later substantiated as actually having occurred.

Usually, when people consider such specific aspects of this type of experience, they concentrate upon the objects that have been seen and the sounds that have been heard. Indeed, that is what was done by the doctor who checked out what a bone saw looked like and those who established the fact that the reported conversation had actually occurred. But there are other questions to be asked: 'Through what eyes did Pam Reynolds see the instrument?' and 'Through what ears did she hear the conversation?' It's all very well the patient speaking about what she saw and heard, but surely one has to ask how it is possible for seeing or hearing to occur at all? If, in ordinary life, somebody says to you: 'I saw so-and-so', or 'I heard so-and-so', you assume that theirs were the eyes that saw or ears that heard. However, in the instance of Pam Reynolds' operation, there is no way such an assumption can be made. Her eyes had been taped shut, and remained inside what was a dead body. One can only conclude that it seems as if 'seeing' can be done without eyes with which to see; and 'hearing' can occur without ears with which to hear. (See also my first book *Seeing Angels*, where I explore in depth reports of visions and hallucinations from blind people who 'saw' but not through their eyes.)

The Pam Reynolds account is by no means the only NDE account proving the survival of consciousness, for there are hundreds in circulation. One that sticks firmly in my mind was documented by Peter and Elizabeth Fenwick in their book *The Truth in the Light*, in which a young man struggled to find adequate words to describe his experience of being him, but not 'in' him:

'... I was aware that I was losing consciousness and of people rushing around me, knocking things over in their efforts to get emergency equipment set up. Then there was nothing; no pain at all. In addition, I was up there on a level with the ceiling. I say, "I was there" because that's how it was. It wasn't a dream; it wasn't imagination. It was as real as me sitting here talking to you. I could actually see myself, me, my body, down there on the bed – I knew it was me down there but it didn't seem to be me if that makes any sense. The me that was really me was up there, out of it all.'

It is times like this when vocabulary becomes insufficient. How can one find words to describe 'the real me'? As the man states, 'the real me' is not his body – but is then lost for words to describe what 'the real me' actually is. Doing his best, he can only come up with: 'The me that was really me was up there', thus implying a split between 'a something' and our bodies.

From the moment of birth, we are all brought up to believe that we are one and the same as the body we abide in. But such NDE and OBE accounts demonstrate that the real body and ourself are not the same. There is something else aside from our bodies and the organs therein. Despite his struggle for words, what this man takes from his experience is unequivocal. He is certain that the 'me that is really me' – whatever it is – is not his body.

I stress that there are hundreds of other well-documented experiences and countless more without documentation.

From all these thoughts can be drawn the general conclusion that we consist of much more than our physical bodies – and that this larger self continues beyond the death of the body. Of course, that claim has been made all through the ages, but the experiences of people such as Pam Reynolds amount to a demonstration of its truth. However, while the claims have long been made, these experiences are in disagreement with most of the teachings that have been handed down to us: not only the teachings of some of the main religions, but also the conclusions that science draws about life.

Since its inception in the middle of the 17th century, science *per se* has been building a body of knowledge of the physical world. Accompanying the acquisition of this body of knowledge, however, has been growing an attitude that the physical world is all there is to know. It is this attitude that is challenged radically by the experience had by Pam Reynolds. After all, her experience suggests strongly that the picture of the world obtained by science is simply not big enough. As she herself said, when reflecting upon her experiences: 'At first I looked for any scientific way of explaining what happened to me. But it soon became clear there simply isn't one.'

Science has been challenged – by this, and many other experiences – to expand its picture so that more than the physical is taken into account. Orthodox scientific teaching does not provide an answer, but there most certainly is a scientific explanation as we have discussed. I remain convinced that it is being blocked or at least actively suppressed.

A similar challenge faces many religions, as their teachings do not fare well in the light of experiences such as that had by Pam Reynolds. In particular, her account contradicts the teachings of orthodox Christianity on what happens to us after death. The ideas of heaven and hell, with the concomitant notions of judgment and salvation, are simply not tenable in the light of her account. At her 'death', Pam Reynolds did not find herself facing a heavenly tribunal who were reviewing the thoughts and deeds of her life in order to arrive at a judgment upon her. Nor did she find herself standing before the throne of the Almighty. Rather, she was, for a time, still present in the operating theatre and observing what the surgeon was doing; and, after that, she was talking with deceased relatives – her grandmother and an uncle who had died young.

After Death Communication (ADC) Experiences

This term, as created by Bill and Judy Guggenheim, is explained in the glossary at the beginning of this book. However, as well as spoken words, some experiences describe 'sensing' the presence of a deceased loved one. In such cases, the experiencer has a certain intuition that a loving presence is close by – or as one lady explained to me: '... suddenly I knew he was there. I could feel his presence. There's no way I can describe it. It was a presence I felt when he was alive, but never noticed that much. It didn't feel strange. It was very natural, like he'd never gone away.' Others describe having a vision of the deceased, seeing them in full or partially, with the clarity ranging from a crystal-clear image to an incomplete, grainy picture. Other common occurrences were audible experiences in which a loved one's voice is heard. Sometimes, it is a one-way communication; at other times, it is two-way. As one widow explained:

'I was thinking of nothing and trying to sleep when the radio sound faded and my husband spoke to me, his voice coming from the radio! He said, "Jenny, are you awake?" I answered and said, "Yes, I'm awake." He said, "Are you all right?" and I said, "Yes." When I realised I was talking to the radio, I was shocked, surprised and panicking to say the least...'

The conversation can vary between being heard externally (as if someone were to talk to you right now) or internally as a sort of telepathic communication. Others have 'felt' the deceased, with accounts ranging from a touch, tap, kiss, hug or caress. One lady wrote: 'Suddenly, I felt two arms wrap around my waist and hug me'. Another, on visiting her aunt's grave, said how she '... felt her arm around my shoulders'.

Making Sense of ADC Experiences

Just think if one were to time travel back to the 17th century and discuss the concept of radio – it would be seen as impossible, even weird for someone to be sitting in a studio and people throughout the country – or even the whole world – being able to hear them at the same time. It would defy logic and go against the grain of science and current understanding – but only of that of the time. Electricity is another example. When it was first discovered, it was seen as miraculous; but now it is just accepted as a day-to-day tool. It is almost as if, after the initial pain of a new idea, the more one gets accustomed to it, then the more natural it seems. I think the same will be the case with materialisation mediumship, mediumship in general and all of the other associated phenomena, such as ADC and so forth.

One of my early memories as a young child was visiting Goonhilly on the Lizard Peninsula in Cornwall while on holiday. There, on Goonhilly Down, is one of the largest satellite earth stations in the world and I remember looking at this vast array of huge satellite dishes filling the landscape. As we stood there, I recall my father trying to explain that even though we couldn't see anything, and even though nothing was moving, these dishes were constantly transmitting information across the world, through space and undersea, fibre-optic cables. At that very moment, as we watched, invisibly, millions and millions of international phone calls, emails and TV broadcasts were somehow being beamed from and to the dishes. I was transfixed, and still remember not quite being able to take it all in. I did not understand how celebrities were beamed from the studio, to this dish, and then into our lounge. We could not see it, but we had the evidence on our television screens and through our radios. These electromagnetic waves are nothing to the naked eye: you can walk through them, stand in front of the dish and they will penetrate you just the same, yet they are able to reform at their destination and depict what they were at their origin.

So, with this in mind, think back to the ghost stories of spirits walking through walls and tables. Then consider this interview with Pat Jeffrey. She told me that during one of the medium Rita Lorraine's experiments a huge easy chair, with a cat asleep on it, was teleported from one room to another. The cat remained asleep when it arrived in the new room. Pat added that they a tremendous job getting the chair back to the correct room the next day! Other sittings have seen 'dead' people walking through furniture and some have explained how they have seen physical objects pushed through other physical objects.

The only way I can visualise these spirits – and indeed ourselves – is as energy. For such we are, in essence, similar to the invisible waves at Goonhilly.

Is it coincidence, then, that Sir Oliver Lodge and Sir William Crookes were both pioneers of radio and television? They knew all about signals and waves and the physics behind them. From this, they were able to put forward a rational explanation to account for the seemingly supernatural phenomena appearing at each of their experiments (whereby deceased loved ones were able to materialise in solid form). In other words, one way of explaining the etheric world is to allude to it being propagated within the same place as radio and television signals – electromagnetic radiation and energy – but at a much higher frequency. It is these recent discoveries in quantum mechanics – the study of the building blocks within the atom and its very constituents – that vindicate entirely what these great physicists said at the beginning of the 20th century?

Ghost Stories

Using the Goonhilly analogy ghosts and stories throughout history suddenly seem to make sense. Perhaps, ghosts seen in old buildings and the like are simply left over memories – good psychometrists are able to pick up on these vibrations. They are like impressions left in the brickwork or atmosphere – marking events that have happened there, like an action replay. This backs up the hearsay from etheric people, 'Everything is recorded on time.' Then there are physical or astral ghosts – ghosts which one sees physically and can at times communicate with. Think back to accounts of ADC from my last book. Some of these figures were only partial materialisations – there were no feet, or only the head and shoulders were visible. These types of ghosts, I believe, are natural materialisations … ectoplasm is drawn from the surroundings by the etheric world and through it the materialisation is able to take place. The same manifestations occur amid physical circles and sittings with the use of a medium. Some circles believe this is ectoplasm is materialised energy; others believe it is a substance or energy extracted from the medium and sitters and, at times, rod-like devices can be felt or pressure over the third eye regions. One circle believes the ectoplasm is then mixed with chemicals by the etheric team – and these can be smelt as they are mixed together.

Auras, Energy and Healing

The human body is a marvellous thing. Its design and engineering are far in advance of anything that we are capable of replicating, despite all our learning, sophistication and technology. No computer, machine or anything has ever come close to it. Damage the body and it will repair itself. Cut your hand and the wound will heal. Our bodies are self-repairing. Yet, as time goes by, slowly we start to loose some of our abilities to self-repair, and our body ages. Eventually, our bodies wear out or are damaged beyond their ability to repair themselves. When this happens, we cast them aside, just as we would cast aside a worn out suit of clothing. Just as we discard worn-out clothing in favour of new clothing, so we cast aside our mortal bodies in favour of our immortal spiritual bodies. The etheric body – our shadow self which surrounds us in our aura – lives on, together with our mind.

There is much we do not yet know or understand as regards the true nature of energy, and it will only be fully understood properly when mediumship and other such phenomena become accepted as natural and totally plausible. Nevertheless, human beings are made up of energy. We are 'energetic beings' and we know that all living things have their own energy field that surrounds them, their 'aura'.

There are many books available which guide you on how to see auras. They include methods which I can only describe as being akin to the 'magic eye pictures' that were rather a craze a short while back. In other words, as one was required to see beyond a seemingly complex visual jumble to discern the true image therein, when looking for an aura, one must look through or beyond the person. At first, all most people can see is a grey envelope around the person, but, with practise, one can develop the seeing of colour. The aura differs from person to person. It is a reflection of physical well-being and so is dependent on their physical and mental state at the time. Sometimes, for some people, the aura can extend considerably beyond the immediate body, with others it can be small and close to the body.

With practise, most people can feel an aura, be it amid a Reiki healing treatment or something else. Then it is possible to feel bumps or blocks, as 'stuck' patches, where the energy doesn't seem to be moving. In fact, it is through Reiki that I have delved deeper into this field and – with no real surprise – I find that the science behind materialisation phenomena agrees perfectly well with it all.

Auras and the Etheric Body
The ether is the first layer surrounding our physical bodies. It is a subtle counterpart of the physical body, which performs two basic functions. The question is open to debate among the various belief systems and philosophies as to whether one's aura and etheric body are synonymous, or related, but different aspects of the energy inherent in human consciousness and the physical body. Whatever, it seems clear that it acts as a battery, or storehouse, for

certain types of vital energies that come from the sun and from the earth (*prana* and *kundalini*, respectively, in Reiki terminology). This energy vitalises the dense physical body, in a way that compliments the energy we receive from the foods we eat. Thereafter, it acts as a bridge of consciousness between the spirit and the body. Specifically, it acts as a bridge of energy and consciousness between the astral body and the physical body.

The etheric vehicle is comprised of matter far more refined and subtle than the simplest of physical matter (the element hydrogen). To the clairvoyant, the etheric vehicle appears as a thin, luminous band of light and energy surrounding the physical body by approximately one inch. It tends to have a silvery-blue-grey colour and varies in intensity and brilliance, depending upon the general health and energy disposition of the individual. It is generally accepted that the aura is layered like an onion, and there are lots of theories about the differing layers. However, it is my belief that there is just one etheric body, like a perfect shadow of our physical body combined with the mind, consciousness, personality or whichever label you wish to adhere to it. Illness and physical exhaustion tend to weaken the etheric vehicle, as do long periods of cloudy weather. On the other hand, good health and vigour cause the etheric vehicle to appear more brilliant and energised.

Anton Mesmer, the father of modern-day hypnosis, conducted a great deal of research on etheric energy-matter. He called it 'animal magnetism'. In his researches, he ascertained that certain people had an abundance of this vital energy-matter. Furthermore, this energy could be transferred, from those who had an abundance of it to those who seemed lacking in it. They could do this through directing this energy mentally as they moved their hands over the individual's aura. He called this type of activity 'magnetic passes' as with the 'laying-on-of-hands' forms of healing, and so on.

Finally, Mesmer discovered that certain people could be placed in a state of sleep, or trance, through such magnetic passes. Then, in that condition, they exhibited paranormal abilities, such as clairvoyance. This was termed 'mesmerism' and, later, became the foundation for hypnosis.

Photographing the Aura – Our Etheric Shadow?
In Moscow, on the 14th October 2003, Russian physicist Dr Konstantine Korotkov stated that he has taken pictures of the soul at the exact moment of dying – offering revolutionary evidence for the debate about the survival of the mind/brain and the etheric body (or soul).

Of late, it has become incredibly popular in New Age circles to 'photograph the aura'. In fact, at many mind, body and spirit festivals and psychic fairs you can have the 'aura' of your hand or body photographed the fee usually includes an interpretation of your emotional state, depending on the colours that surround you. This photography employs high-voltage alternating currents and results from the recording of electrical discharges on film. One of the most popular images in books and articles about this Kirlian photography is the so-called 'phantom leaf'. After a part of a leaf has been cut off, a phantom of the missing part still appears in the Kirlian image. This is a remarkable result, and would suggest that it might also be possible to photograph phantom limbs, fingers, and so on.

In cases of materialisations and one-off ghostly

apparitions or ADC, we know the deceased revert to a state that is not necessarily that of the manner in which they died. For example, victims mutilated in a traffic accident, or people who had lost a limb in their lives, often choose to reappear as they were in their prime, while still indicating how they know they will be recognised.

However, as Rupert Sheldrake points out, there may be serious hindrances to the leaf experiment[11]. The phantom leaf effect can arise by means of a simple error. If the operator first puts the leaf on the film and then cuts off part of it, this leaves a damp impression of the missing part. The image on the photograph simply arises from this dampness on the film. Even pieces of damp blotting paper have an 'aura' in a Kirlian photograph; when the blotting paper is placed upon the film and parts are then cut off, images of 'phantom' blotting paper appear in photographs.

Having said that, although some 'phantom leaf' images have been accidentally produced in this way, images of phantoms can still appear when the leaf is cut *before* being placed on the film; but not always, as the effect is elusive. While some practitioners can obtain phantom images relatively frequently, others do so rarely or not at all.

Several attempts have already been made to detect phantom limbs and fingers by this method, but so far without success. So, although the prospects for this new line of research are not too hopeful, it might be worth a few more tries. For example, it would be interesting to see an aura photograph of an amputee.

Now, having examined all of the topics associated with materialisation and so forth, it is time to look at some genuine, witnessed experiences.

7

DEVELOPING
PHYSICAL MEDIUMSHIP:
SOME CASE STUDIES

'I did not say it was possible, I said it happened.'

SIR WILLIAM CROOKES.

THE CREATION OF PHYSICAL phenomena and partial and complete materialisations is an incredibly rare form of mediumship. Indeed, as I write, the number of strong developing physical mediums in the UK can be counted on one hand; and those known about in the rest of the world can be counted on two hands. It is incredibly rare in occurrence; but just because something is rare does not mean it cannot be proven or does not exist.

Until around the 1930s physical mediumship was very common, and the strength and range of phenomena were amazing. So why, today, it is so uncommon? There are two basic reasons.

First, it has been argued that physical mediums have an excess of ectoplasmic energy in their body. To some degree, most people have this energy, but in very small quantities.

Second, in the early days, when the 'modern' type of spirit phenomena were relatively new, people wanted objective evidence that it was happening; and this resulted in the preponderance of physical manifestations. As people began accepting the reality of mediumship, and then yearning more for teaching and philosophy, the occurrence of physical mediumship began to lessen, while mental mediumship began to predominate. In other words, the needs of humanity seemed to dictate how the etheric people would respond.

It is also worth noting that the development of physical mediumship can be a lengthy process, sometimes tedious, with nothing happening in the circle for months or even years. It requires great commitment on everyone's part, and generally revolves around the development of one – maybe two – people in the circle, with the other people sitting to help them in their development. Yet, one circle with which I have been in touch has been sitting regularly for over 14 years, and their development during that time has been phenomenal.

In addition, today, unlike much of the 20th century, other commitments prevail. It seems that people are just not geared to putting in the necessary time and effort – sometimes totally selflessly – into the development of any form of mediumship. In contrast, in earlier years, sitting in a circle was often what people did to socialise. Most of the great pioneer mediums began by sitting in a home circle. Today, this is simply not the case; other home entertainments are more common, and the home is no longer the heart of the family that it once was. So, much of this can be blamed on a simple change in lifestyle.

Whatever the causes, the occurrence, as well as the nature, of physical mediumship is nothing like it was a century ago. However, since the 1990s, there seems to have been a resurgence of interest in physical mediumship and, consequently, resurgence in the development of physical mediums. Where this will lead, only time will tell.

Three Contemporary Experiments

Perhaps the best way of understanding the processes, occurrences and associated phenomena of developing mediums is to consider accounts of some recent experiments or sittings for what they can reveal and teach us. These involve two contemporary groups – Circles A and Patrick McNamara and the ghostcircle. I think if they continue to strengthen and develop, then I would hope, given much time and patience, they will become as good as some of the past physical mediums.

Contemporary Experiment 1 – Patrick McNamara and the Ghostcircle

The following is an account by Karl Fallon from a circle that has been sitting for about eight years with ten to twelve regular members. On the night in question, in February 2004, the circle was working with a developing medium. There were two guest sitters and seven group members present. What follows is his description of the evening.

The group assembles as usual on the evening of the circle. The room is arranged in the same way and the chairs and table are laid out in the same format each week. The table is a small fold-down type with castor wheels. In its centre is placed a speaking trumpet with some luminous strips. All windows are locked and blacked out to prevent any light intruding from the street outside; a glass of water and an empty glass are placed on opposite sides of the room for use by the spirit guide; in the corner of the room is a red light which the medium controls as needs be; above the circle is a chandelier with red and blue light bulbs controlled by a dimmer switch. No cabinet is currently used for ectoplasm formations but a night-vision, infrared camera, running on battery power only, is set up in one corner of the room to record any activity.

The circle is composed of male and female members, the majority being female. There is one door in and out. Once the members are seated, the doors are closed outside the room and all the lights are switched off. The door is closed firmly but not locked. All members know each other very well. The medium is the last to be seated to make sure everything is ready, and is located at the top of the table. There is total darkness. The medium leads the introduction, which always starts with everyone joining hands and saying the Lord's Prayer. This is always done for protective reasons, although the circle is totally secular in its approach.

After the prayer, the first part of the circle begins. There is an electrical charge in the air, which people can feel by moving their hands about them. Some people are already feeling ectoplasm as it falls on their face. Some members are feeling cold breezes around them, although all windows and doors are closed and the room is warm from the central heating.

The first part of the circle is a healing section. This is used for three reasons: it helps people relax and switch off from any daily stress that they may have had; it sends out healing prayers to those who need them; and it harmonises the circle members.

The second part begins once the healing is completed, but we break our hands briefly and stretch before it begins. The medium continues by asking the members to join fingertips on the table. The speaking trumpet is on the table and the luminous bands around it is the only light to be seen. The new members comment on how the top of the trumpet keeps disappearing, as if somebody is walking in front of it. It resembles a lighthouse effect. One member has been touched on the head. We can all feel cold breezes around our feet – this is where the energy is building up.

The red light in the corner is switched on. The medium starts to give clairvoyance to the additional members. As he gives some evidence to the members, he is partially taken over by the father of one sitter and briefly takes on his personality, saying in an American accent: 'Ah, I don't care, I'm doing it anyway.' The medium regains control and pushes the father back out of his body. The member laughs and says: 'It was just like he would have been, pushy and impatient!' We all laugh.

Names and personal incidents are given and taken as correct. To be frank, he tells the member that her father was a no good, heavy-drinking womaniser. He had many affairs, loved gambling and talked about Las Vegas. He was a man's man. All of this she accepts as being very true. This is all very accurate evidence, and the member adds that the voice that had come through the medium, albeit briefly, was immediately recognisable as the way he spoke on earth. She says, 'That's my dad.'

Later, as the table moves about, it is asked if the member's father could be doing the moving – at which point the table bounces around on two legs even one leg at times to show he is still a very forceful domineering person. This goes on for about a couple of minutes with encouragement from the circle. As the evidence is given, the member has no qualms about the truth of her father being revealed. Other members give clairvoyance to each other, while the medium concentrates with evidential proof on the new members. The energy has built up enough for the medium to try some physical manifestation. As stated earlier, no cabinet is in use in order to use a new form of ectoplasm that can be seen clearly in the red light.

On this particular evening, the medium asks us all to put our hands flat on the table. We are told to look at our fingertips. The fingers on the hands seem to be growing. In fact, lines of grey and blue light can be seen from the fingers of the individual members of the circle, not only can we see the lights, but we can also feel the energy coming from it. It seems to form small clouds. Individual fingers grew longer, some grow shorter. The table jolts beneath our hands and starts to move in the direction of the new members of the circle. The medium says, 'If you look closely at the clouds of ectoplasm beginning to form, you will see faces in them.'

The table continues to move under our hands and a charge of static electricity forms on our faces like cobwebs. This is the ectoplasm in the atmosphere. The medium tells us to be aware that we will be touched. Some members are then touched. As this is happening, the lower halves of our bodies are being submerged in what feels like cold water. Across the surface of the table there are more cold draughts hitting our hands as they lie there, touching a member's hand each side. The red light is still the only light on, and no doors or windows are open; we can clearly see what is going on in the circle. The medium then says to observe him closely as he walks over to the corner of the room and switches on the overhead chandelier, so that the room is very illuminated with the red and blue light.

The medium turns and as he walks across the room slowly, a figure arises from the floor bedside him and forms the shape of a man. This is a shadow constructed of light. It seems to detach itself from the medium and, as he walks around the circle, can be seen attached to the medium's back. As he approaches one side of the room, one of the newer members can see the face of her mother in a cloud that seems to be issuing from another member of the circle.

The medium then gives the name of the person with him, which is accepted as being correct. The medium returns to his seat and the spirit with him seems to recede slowly. The table starts to move quite briskly and the trumpet, still sitting on the table glides back and forth.

The medium then says that the lights will be turned off completely. The chandelier and corner light are extinguished. He then asks all members to join hands. We have a feeling of rest, warmth, and completeness as we sit there. The medium asks us to look upwards to see all the spirit lights above our heads, which represents all the spirits who are present tonight. We sit for a few moments, and the medium says that we will close for the evening. We are asked one last time to put our hands on the table. The medium goes over and turns on the chandelier light again, as we look up we can see that the metal arms seem to be moving like waves shaking above us.

We start to close down individually and a closing prayer is said. Once this is done we have tea and refreshments as normal. Then, in normal light, a strange thing starts to happen. The medium says that some members will start to change colour, one by one; each person has a different colour on their face, as the spirits use up some of the remaining energy. One face is a light green, another orange, and another blue. This only lasts a few minutes. The light is normal white light – the coloured ones have been switched off. We then have a discussion about the night's events.

Contemporary Experiment 2 – Circle A

This following account was written by a colleague, Montague Keen, who sadly passed over whilst I was completing the final manuscript. He attended a sitting with a developing physical medium on Saturday 25 October 2003 in the UK. During the experiment, both Montague and his wife experienced 'a variety of movements and touches, noises and voices ... in circumstances which appeared to preclude fraud.'

Many precautions were taken before and during the

experiment and Montague's conclusion, despite reasonable familiarity with the past history of comparable demonstrations, was that the effects seemed genuine. His description follows.

The sitting took place in the home of a friend of the medium (known hereon as 'the host'). My attendance was consequent on a personal introduction, supported by a good relationship of trust with the host, following his important evidential contribution to the Scole Report[a]. Together with my wife and myself, and the host, it was attended by the circle leader, the medium and his wife, and about ten or twelve others.

The room used was in a small block a few feet from the bungalow of the host, and was entered via an anteroom, where all those attending were asked to leave behind loose jewellery, handbags, watches, pens, wallets, money: indeed anything which could be detached. For this purpose everyone was searched, although I was allowed to bring in a notebook and pen, which was left under the chair of my immediate neighbour, until he had an opportunity, during the experiment, to ask whether permission would be granted by the etheric people for me to use it. (It was duly granted, but the pen could not easily be found in the darkness, so the idea was abandoned.)

I searched the medium and ascertained there was nothing in any trouser pockets or concealed on his singlet, over which he wore a cardigan, which I searched separately before he replaced it. I also checked his trainer-type shoes to ascertain that the heels and soles were normal and unified.

There was only one door into the séance room, which had no windows. The room measured roughly 15 feet by 9 feet 6 inches. It was perfectly rectangular except for a recess (4 feet by 2 feet by 7 feet high) at one end, itself devoid of ornaments or further recesses. By the recess there was a rectangular curtain rail from which three floor-length black curtains were suspended by Velcro straps, so that the curtains could be opened and closed from both sides. This, along with the recess, constituted the cabinet. The room was seamlessly carpeted throughout. Apart from the entrance door from the anteroom, there were no detectable orifices beyond five small vents in the ceiling and three low-level vents along one wall, vented to the outside. Moulded plastic seats were placed around all the walls, save the cabinet end. Two of the seats blocked the entrance door, and that occupied by my wife prevented the door from being opened.

The chair (owned by the host), in which the medium sat, was an old-fashioned upholstered, heavy, wooden construction. This I examined carefully in view of a claim by the magician Ian Rowland: when he was commenting on television about this medium's reputed feats, he said that if the ends of the chair arms were not securely connected to the posts, the medium could raise his arms from the post and slip the cable ties off his arms. (This is a suggestion I will examine later.) I could find no loose connections, and was unable to move the arms or see or feel anything abnormal underneath the chair.

The chair was placed inside the open cabinet, and the medium was strapped into it by means of plastic tree ties. This was effected by the medium's wife, under my close supervision. I was invited to examine the ties, which were already permanently fixed to the legs and arms of the chair, both before and after the fixing. Straps were placed through these permanent fixings, and pulled tight, and then secured with thin plastic ties with the ends trimmed off, so that the only way to release the bond was to cut it. The straps were so tightly pulled that I was unable to intrude even a finger. Indeed, the medium subsequently was heard to complain that his wife had been so enthusiastic as to cause him discomfort. A black gag was tied securely round the medium's head through his open mouth, thereby preventing normal speech. I examined the gag and the knot behind the head. Finally, the several buttons on the front of medium's cardigan were tied into the buttonholes with thin strips of black plastic. These one-way (self-locking) cable ties are incapable of being untied. They have to be cut to be released.

On the floor, a few feet in front of the medium, there was a black-coated piece of board, about 3 feet 6 inches by 2 feet. After I had checked underneath (prompted by the host) to satisfy myself that nothing was concealed below it, the following items were placed on it: a cardboard trumpet, the end of which was coated with luminous paint; a mouth organ; a rattle; and two drumsticks, all of which were to play a part in the sitting. In addition, there were a pair of pliers, which was employed by the medium's wife to cut the ties to release her husband after the sitting, and two wooden rings, which were brought into the room from the anteroom by the host at the medium's request, after my wife had taken a number of photographs.

A microphone (an Optimus 33-3013) was suspended from the wall near the door, the other end being connected to a Sony personal cassette-style tape-recorder, located on a small table next to the host. He switched on the machine and turned over the cassette tape after it had automatically switched off on reaching the end of one side. Copies of the tape recording were freely available to any participant requesting it by sending a blank tape to the host.

The only other equipment was a small flexible table lamp with a red bulb and fixed shade. It was placed on a small table in the corner on the medium's left, outside the curtain, together with a glass of water. In the opposite corner was a large a tape recorder playing music. The light was controlled by the circle leader, who sat alongside me, while the music player was the responsibility of the medium's wife, who had to make frequent changes in the music and the volume, at the behest of etheric communicators. Both the circle leader's hands held my right hand throughout the sitting, save for about five minutes when they were needed to switch on and manoeuvre the light during the brief period when ectoplasmic extrusions were being shown.

Before the sitting, when all participants were seated on cushioned chairs against the three walls, the circle leader enjoined everyone to remain still, not to grasp at anything unless permission was sought and granted. He explained the dangers to which the medium was exposed – should anyone make an unauthorised grab at any ectoplasmic extension – and emphasised the importance of keeping our arms still: advice echoed and amplified by communicators in response to later questions. The lights were then dimmed to disappearance. The dimmer control knob was removed from the wall-mounted dimmer switch, and the remainder of the box was taped over by the host.

The sitting began with a short prayer offered by one of the sitters. This was followed, not by normally rousing music but, rather to my surprise, by Pachelbel's 'Canon', to which we were invited to sing along; and then, no less surprisingly, by the distinctly menacing dance of the courtiers from Prokofiev's 'Romeo and Juliet'. Thereafter more popular music was played, but frequently altered in volume at the behest of one or other communicator.

At the end of the sitting, following the withdrawal of the final communicator, the host stripped the sealer tape from the light switch and restored the dimmer control knob to enable the light to be slowly turned up. It revealed the medium still tied to his chair, and gagged, in the middle of the room, some seven or eight feet from his original position inside the cabinet. The chair had been moved over the top of the black board and its several instruments. When the medium had recovered sufficiently to face the light, and the gag had been removed and retied to shield his eyes from the flashes, my wife took a number of post-sitting photographs. These included one showing the cardigan reversed. Having checked that the ties were still in place, I watched as his wife used the pliers to cut each off the ties fixing

the buttons to the buttonholes, and I examined the arm
and leg bindings as she cut the ties to enable the straps
to be unfastened.

Let me now summarise the physical events that I
experienced personally, or that I also witnessed with the
rest of the participants:

1. The translocation to a different part of the room of the
medium bound in his chair.

2. The reversal of the medium's cardigan, without the
plastic ties being broken.

3. The trumpet, the luminous large end of which was
seen to be performing a variety of patterns and aerial
adornments, was operated at great speed and with
considerable precision, and was pressed quite hard
against my chest at one stage.4. My head was tapped
sharply several times, apparently by the luminous end of
the trumpet during the aerial demonstrations.

5. I was vigorously slapped on both knees as an
introduction to the first supposedly materialised entity.

6. My tie was unknotted, ripped off, and thrust with great
precision in the narrow space between the chairs on
which my wife and I were sitting. It was later found on the
carpet beneath the chairs.

7. The two rings of equal dimensions but different woods
were found on the left arm of one of the sitters, sitting
opposite me and alongside the medium's wife. Towards
the end of the sitting, he had reported that someone was
trying to force the rings over his wrist. When I tried to pull
them over his hand to remove them, he complained that
it was painful, although later succeeded in doing so. He
contrasted this with the relatively gentle pressure

experienced when the rings had been were pushed over his wrist during the sitting.

8. While I was holding my wife's right hand with my left, leaving my index finger protruding, we were both touched by a warm, soft and seemingly human hand for about 15 seconds.

9. There was tap-dancing of an apparently expert kind, as well as extremely fast drumming on the ceiling during the Irish jig music.

10. A silver tie-pin surmounted by a cat was apported as a gift to the medium's wife, purportedly through the mouth of the medium as he extruded ectoplasm.

11. We heard a very clear, loud and distinctive series of four voices we heard, all of which answered questions intelligently.

The evening was notable for the clarity and fluency of the two principal communicators, who introduced themselves as William Charles Cadwell (died 1897) and Sir William Crookes, both of whom invited and answered questions. Two other voices familiar to the regular participants also came through: a cockney youth named Timothy Booth, and Louis Armstrong. Both had very distinctive features and claimed to have materialised. Timothy was responsible for the widespread reports of touches and boisterous noises, as well as the delicate management of the ectoplasm and the ordering of the correct degree of red light to enable us to see the medium but not harm him.

Below is an edited account of the entire séance for the record. Despite its necessary length, each virtually verbatim account, based on the tape recording, highlights the interesting aspects of mediumship phenomena and ontological issues. I have usually omitted such phrases as 'my dear friends', 'of course', and similar adornments.

Cadwell came through very soon after the introductory music stopped and talked in a clear, elderly and precise voice (not dissimilar to that of Crookes, who spoke much later, apart from the impediment Cadwell had in rolling his Rs). Cadwell described himself as a guide and mentor to the medium and expressed an interest in me as 'some would say, an understanding scientist.' [I expressed modest gratification] He said that they (his etheric associates) would 'endeavour to prove to you that life exists beyond death.' He urged us all to follow the circle leader's guidelines for the protection of the medium and of the circle itself. He invited questions. When permission was sought for me to make notes, he gave approval, provided I held the notebook neatly against my torso; he then withdrew into the cabinet for a few moments, accompanied by a whooshing sound, and then proceeded to invite questions.

I asked how the voice was produced, and how far it used the medium's larynx, or how far it was direct voice. This was his response:

'Well, I could describe it to you now that I myself am partly materialised. The ectoplasm is exuded from the medium's body by various orifices and is moulded around the young man's voice box to create a larynx effect, but I myself am speaking to you with my own voice: placing myself within the ectoplasm exuded from the medium's body by means of coating the etheric body of the ectoplasm, you understand?' [Yes] 'And I am then able to speak. There is at some point during the séance when the materialisation of form is not taking place and it is merely that of independent direct voice. You understand?' [Yes] 'But I myself partly materialise.' [Thank you very much]

We continued as follows:

MK: Do you feel you have moved into the room, or are you still at your point of departure?

A: I hope that I am in the room; otherwise I'm in the wrong place. [Laughter]

MK: You feel that you have moved?

A: Yes my friend: I feel as solid as solid can be. [Thank you] So many people; so few questions...

MK: Well, perhaps I could ask again. You say you feel solid, but you are in fact a creation of your own mind: is that not the case?

A: If I could describe to you this: due to the vibration of young David that is emanating from his physical body, I am able to interpenetrate that of the earth's vibration by means of my etheric body vibration changes. I am then able to coat myself into a physical ectoplasmic form; then I am able to be here within the earth environment; but when the energy depletes it is much more difficult for materialisation and communication to take place, so the need is for the energy to be produced, so often by yourselves, to help the energy of the young man within the chair: to substantiate[a] the energy levels and keep them at such a level that I myself and others are able to commune. You understand?

MK: In so far as any such communication can make

117

sense of our limited capacity to envisage a different world, and a different means of communications, as it does – it is very difficult …

A: As it is for me to describe absolutely what is taking place: it is quite a process that is more than what I have explained: you understand.

The voice then urged us to hold hands for a moment.

A: 'I shall show you something. What is your name, sir?

MK: Mine? Montague.

A: Good evening. [… I was then slapped vigorously on my right knee

MK: I was heartily slapped on my … oh again [on my left knee] with a very solid feeling. Thank you!

A: You may now release hands. Now you see how … materialisation within the earth's vibration by means of ectoplasm? [Indeed]

MK: Why, when we held hands there, did that make it easier for you to demonstrate that?

A: It helps the energy to be built up to greater levels, but also it is for the safety of the medium and the ectoplasmic structure. Quite often when people are touched they feel the need to touch back or flee from whatever: so it may be safety as well, you understand.

MK: You mentioned the energy being heightened by holding hands. Is that what would have possibly enabled Mr Webber[2] to work without a cabinet during his mediumship, because I think they held hands throughout the whole sitting.

A: Yes, that is correct.

MK: So it is possible to work without a cabinet?

A: May be in time to come. When [this medium] is

more developed in his physical mediumship, we aim to dispense with the cabinet, and there have been times in the past when this would have been possible, but you must understand that any emotional or psychological change within the medium has an affect upon the energy levels and also affects that of the physical manifestation. [Right]

MK: So that, therefore, it would be beneficial for those in development to sit within a cabinet rather than ...?

A: Yes, of course, in the early stages. The cabinet is used to allow us to keep the energy close to the medium, but also for the ectoplasm to be manipulated far more easily for materialisation to take place.

MK: Is it going to be possible for the medium here to actually produce physical phenomena in some sort of light?

A: Recently photographs of ectoplasm have been taken in red light... We shall endeavour this evening to produce ectoplasm that can be seen in red light. This will be the first time it has been done outside the environment where the home circle is normally conducted. So it will be a first: it will be your [the host's] sanctuary where we wish to do this.

Host: An honour and a privilege, William; thank you. I then went on to ask about the use of infrared photography.

MK: May I ask another question: this anticipates some of the inevitable queries by my more sceptical colleagues who are always insistent that, despite the elaborate precautions taken to avoid any form of deception, they would still like to have infrared photography through a video: we have never quite understood what the technical objections are to this. Would you be prepared to elaborate?

A: I understand. Any form of electrical equipment that is used for infrared photographic images of any sort does exude a type of ray, I believe the right word is, but of what consistency I do not know. But this type of ray that is exuded from the photographical equipment has a burning sensation upon the ectoplasm. It is a little like placing the hand in sulphuric acid. But as mediumship progresses in time there will be no need for infrared photography because all will be seen in spirit-induced light or that of red light if possible so that, as sceptical as your colleagues may be, they cannot be sceptical when the medium is firmly strapped in the chair and a materialised form is seen to be standing in the room.

MK: If I may say so, with great respect, you'd be surprised how far scepticism is sometimes taken.

A: Of course, there will always be those to whom you cannot prove no matter what you do. Within your field you will always have those who believe or wish to believe, and those who do not. This is a fact of life.

MK: Unfortunately this is too true.

My wife asked whether there was anything she could tell her sister in order to help her when she was so frightened of dying.

A: Convey to her this: to pass into the spirit (etheric) vibration is a glorious reunion of souls that have passed before. It is nothing for your sister to be frightened of: it is a changing of vibrations –from those of the earth to those of the spirit vibrations. Quite often people are retarded because of their religious belief that they are going to some place of eternal sleep and, of course, in the initial stages of entering the spirit dimension, they themselves might feel the necessity to sleep, and quite often these people wake up and wonder what they are doing when they have no physical body to sustain them any more; and when this occurs, it is quite often that clergyman of their chosen religion will go visit them and speak to them and explain that there was certainly eternal sleep. Now, if I remember right, Mr Leslie Flint, who was a direct voice medium, produced a tape by Dr Cosmo Lang who was the Archbishop of Canterbury, and who returned and said, 'Of course life goes on, and I was wrong in my assumptions while I was here upon the physical plane.' My great friend Dr Theobald Slawinsky who is a cardio-vascular surgeon and works with [this medium] in the state of trance for the purpose of healing and psychic surgery, would be more than happy to visit your dear sister, and if he is able to help, of course he will. [Thank you very much] Be assured there is nothing to fear.

It seemed about time to raise the reincarnation issue, and this I did.

MK: There are some schools of thought that say that the earth plane is a plane of individualisation. I was trying to sort out in my mind whether this individuality, once established on the earth plane remains in the person's consciousness once they are in spirit.

A: It depends whether you believe in reincarnation, and [this medium] is open-minded, as you may know. I myself wholeheartedly believe in the fact of reincarnation. I believe this: this is just my interpretation, that when we pass to the world of spirit we obviously still retain our personality, and upon the transition through the spheres of living within the world of spirit you start to lose that identity of the earth's environment and the consciousness that you had, but it cannot be totally eradicated, and when the time of reincarnation takes place, there is always an essence of that of what you were, and this is quite often how, when some people are regressed, they are able to bring forward past memories. It would be, and it is, quite foolhardy of me to say this: that all thoughts are eradicated, but you must understand that like [this medium], who is open-minded about the fact of reincarnation, he himself would find it very difficult under a state of hypnosis to bring forward any past life experience. This is due to himself being open-minded, but more so of the fact of being disbelieving of the fact of reincarnation. So it could be firmly embedded in his subconscious mind that it would be detrimental to his thoughts and his emotions – if you can imagine: quite often people who have had difficult childhoods – they hide from every fact within the recesses of the subconscious mind, do they not? So much for past life experiences. No matter how hard you try, you are unable to bring forward that what it is. I hope that answers your question. [Thank you, chorus] I must go now. A pleasure to have been speaking to you; maybe I'll speak to some more people at another time. Good evening to you. [Good evening]

Music was then used again and we all joined in singing the hymn 'Jerusalem', after which a squeaky voice was heard. This was followed by an Irish jig, accompanied by clapping sticks in strict time to the music, then a more vigorous jig to which something appeared to be dancing and clapping materialised hands. 'Banging on the ceiling,' said my wife, amid much noise.

The trumpet's luminous tip was flashing around the room and periodically touching sitters. When the music ceased, amid cries of 'well done', another less energetic tune followed, and a small voice said: 'Turn it off', at which point the medium's wife switched off the music, and Tim introduced himself.

After some light-hearted badinage with the host, Tim explained in a high-pitched, artificially baby-like voice that it was his job to make the ectoplasm come out.[4] He asked whether he should materialise, which he was encouraged to do. Then he said he needed a bit more ectoplasm, and urged us to hold on. There was a whooshing sound of a strangulated type, and a sudden scream of childish laughter.

The host said he had missed the board [with his jump from the cabinet]. Tim complained that it had been put a long way away [from the medium][5] and the circle leader commented, 'Just testing you'. The host then quipped, 'Mind you don't twist your ankle!' and the to and fro continued.

Tim: No need to test me, Buzzy Boy[6].

The host: Timothy, when you had the trumpet up, it would seem that separate from that – I don't know whether anyone else noticed – but I did see quite a few sort of flashes. Is that something you were experimenting with?

Tim: They were spirit lights we were hoping to bring eventually. Did everybody see them? [No] You must be blind, then! [General laughter accompanied by a high-pitched cackle from Tim]

The host: It was very, very quick and subtle, like a glow of energy rather than a pinpoint of light, but it was definitely separate from the trumpet.

Tim: D'you know what we're going to do tonight? You've got choices. If you want to see ectoplasm in red light, we won't be able to bring in any loved ones. We haven't quite mastered doing both.

The consensus of opinion was sought by the circle leader. The red light was decided upon and Tim commented: 'We can do most things but we can't work miracles.' [Another cackle] He asked whether anyone was frightened. Was my companion my wife?

I confirmed this, and said she was nervous only when he laughed. He urged her not to be frightened and assured her she would not be hurt – may be a little bit. [More laughter] He then asked everyone to listen because he had fully materialised. There were sounds of something walking about; my wife let out a short scream as she was touched on the knee. Then, both her right and my left hand, holding one another, were fondled for several seconds by what seemed to be a small hand, quite soft and warm. Paul, on my left, said that both his hands were holding my right hand, and the man on my wife's left confirmed that he had been holding her left hand throughout, all the more tightly because she was clearly nervous.

Tim asked whether we had heard his footsteps: 'You

see, I materialised partly, then'. When he complained that we were a very quiet lot tonight, I commented that we were awestruck, and Tim remarked that oars were used for boats. [Cackle] He appeared to require more ectoplasm and said we could release hands for the moment. The host said he had seen a fairly bright light in front of him, but it seemed to have gone. It stayed in the same place even when he moved his head. Tim explained that they were creating an energy field around the room.

Tim then addressed 'Mrs Monty' and asked whether she had a camera – a new-fangled one. My wife said she had, and Tim confirmed that, at the end of the sitting but before the medium was cut out of the chair, she could take a couple of photographs, if that was all right with the circle leader. The circle leader sought further guidance and suggested it would be better if the pictures were taken when the medium had been released and had been given some water, but Tim said it ought to be done when he was still bound. The medium would say when he was awake.

Tim then announced that he would bring an apport for the medium's wife. She promised she would wear it all the time. My wife asked where he got the apport from. He said he would have to seek permission to tell her. There was a short pause; then he announced that he had been given permission. He said there was a stall halfway down the Portobello Road[7] that sold curios. He thought it was called Jan or Jane's Curios – or something like that. 'We borrowed it off of her.' [Laughter] 'We asked her mum in the spirit world if she would mind and she said she won't even miss it – but she did, you know: she was looking for it to try and find it!' [Cackle] 'And just to make it more interesting, when we switch the red light on, we'll try and materialise it: we'll apport it out of his mouth, shall we?' [Chorus of assent] 'We'll materialise it in the ectoplasm and try bringing it out of his mouth.'

When the host pointed out that the medium had a gag in his mouth, and implied that this might make things difficult, Tim said, 'You'd be surprised. He's got a big mouth.' [Laughter and cackle] He said they might need music to enable them to do what they had to do. He would let us know when he was ready.

After a brief interrogation about the curtains and lights, and whether the music should be played throughout, Tim promised to make a bang when they were ready. He didn't want the red light too low or too high because they (the spirits) had never attempted this before, explaining that they might see the medium's face contort a little. We asked him whether he could knock three times to ensure that we knew when he was ready, to which he responded, amid laughter, by singing a line from the old pop song: 'Knock three times on the ceiling if you want me...'

Music was re-started. We joined in singing Sting's 'An Englishman in New York'. The circle leader then asked for the music to stop and everyone to remain absolutely quiet. I was asked to turn on the wall switch governing the red lamp. There followed much manoeuvring while the curtain on my side was opened and the light, pointing downwards to avoid shining in the medium's face, was adjusted. The medium's wife checked to ensure everyone could see the medium. We then saw a white substance stretching from the medium's face and across his chest to his lap.

After about half a minute Tim asked for the light to be turned off at the main switch and the music resumed. Tim explained that the music and singing were needed to generate the energy, a lot of which was needed for this sort of demonstration. He asked the host when was the last time he had seen ectoplasm. The host replied that it was about three years ago in a sitting with another physical medium. Since then, some 300 people had attended his séances.

Addressing me as 'Uncle Monty', Tim asked for my reactions. I wondered what had become of the ectoplasm. Tim said it had been dematerialised: it was dangerous when the ectoplasm was out of the medium. He had kept a little bit for himself to enable him to talk to us. This was the first time they had brought through an apport via the ectoplasm with the red light on: it was dangerous. My wife described a light she saw in front of her. The host said it was the same as the light he saw.

Tim asked me whether my wife usually saw such things. I said she did, but I did not. Tim observed, amid laughter, that, 'If your missus sees things, it's got to be true' – followed by another cackle. He called for music. It was switched on. I did not see the apport being produced, but it was on the floor near the medium's wife when the séance ended.

The music then played a Louis Armstrong song, 'What A Wonderful World'. Armstrong's voice was heard on the tape, and then a voice, apparently identical to

Armstrong's, accompanied it. It was quite clear. This was followed by the voice introducing himself.

'How are all you fine people here this evening? May I introduce myself? My name is Louis Armstrong' [expressions of welcome], known by many as Satchmo. I've got to say this is very difficult speaking through this here voice box.' [murmurs of sympathy and encouragement]

The medium's wife sought permission to pose a question and received the reply: 'Yes you can ask me a question if you wish, my dear.' She said she had lost a tape with Satchmo singing with a lady, and she could not find it.

'Well, my dear, you've got the record at home.'

She expressed gratification.

'So you didn't have to look that far did you?' [pause] 'I'm just going to materialise.'

There followed a whooshing noise followed by the sound of a minor collision. I commented that he'd tripped over something.

'No I haven't my friend. I'm just showing you I've materialised.'

There followed several knocks and bangs, and it became clear it was some sort of soft shoe shuffle.

'There you are my friends, and I bid you good night.'

The voice was loud, clear and highly idiosyncratic, immediately recognisable as Satchmo's uniquely guttural pronunciation. After a pause, we heard some heavy breathing sounds, and a very croaky voice, which shortly became firmer and addressed us. We welcomed him. We were asked to keep talking to help the vibrations.

The circle leader greeted him, and the voice asked everyone to sit still: 'I wish to fully materialise...' He then introduced himself as Sir William Crookes. 'Some of you may know me from my scientific research, but some of you by means of my communication and friendship with the physical medium Florence Cook. At no time was there any doubt in my mind of any fraud or of Miss Cook. [Comment from the host: 'There are quite a few photographs showing Florence and Katie (King) separately.']

'There are two reasons why I came to this gathering this evening. One was purely to make my presence felt here and to commune with people of like minds. One was also because of my interest in this young man's mediumship. As you have seen this evening, ectoplasm was exuded from this young man in red light and seen, and as you know I myself witnessed full materialisation in light, that of the materialised form of Kate King. Are you all familiar with this? [general assent] I shall endeavour to move further into the room. Now I am sure there are those among you who may have questions of me. Please feel free to ask and I shall endeavour to answer.'

I asked whether those guilty of unfair opposition and criticism during his lifetime had now recanted in the afterlife.

He replied, 'I would not say they have recanted. I would say their minds have been firmly changed.'

He asked my name, and I told him.

'Ah, so you're Keen are you? I have heard words of you, I can tell you, dear boy. I understand you are going to endeavour to continue some of the work that I started'. [We are] 'Well carry on the good work, dear boy.'

I commented, 'Your work was an inspiration to us and many others.'

He replied, 'I was not swayed, dear friend, by any means.'

I then quoted his own words: 'I did not say that it was possible; I simply said that it happened.'

At this point, I felt my tie being unknotted. I commented on this, saying that the hands unknotting it were firm: 'My tie is now being pulled out and I think undone by firm hands. Thank you. Both my hands are being held and – ah! My tie is being taken off! I hope it won't dematerialise.'

'As you can see, my friend, anything is possible,' the voice resumed. 'Let me explain something in regard to external energies being brought into the séance room. Some of you may know I myself was a party to developing vacuum tubes which were part of X-ray tubes, you understand. Do you know of this Keen. [I do, sir] 'Well you will know that X-ray is something which exudes energy, does it not? Well, within the séance room the energy is in heightened state, and bringing into the séance room any form of electricity other than that that is compensated for, which sometimes proves to be quite difficult to work with, can have a disastrous effect on the mediumship of the individual within the chair. When I witnessed the materialisation of Katie King, that was the most thought-provoking change in my life. It was at that time that the reality of life after death really touched my soul. Then there was no going back. Then I had to bring to the world the truth of the continuity of life. Now I would say this to you: put away your electrical equipment of infrared status for this young man and other physical mediums, manifestations will be seen again in that sort of light produced either by the spirit vibrations or by that of your own means, if we allow it in the séance room. That is all I have to say.'

There then followed a question and answer conversation:

Q: When working with the medium you worked with, did you witness her materialise from nothing, or from scratch basically to full form, or did you just witness her coming out of the cabinet?

A: At one time I was privileged to see ectoplasm exuding from the medium's body by means of the mouth and solar plexus, and from this even what seemed to be ectoplasm on the floor in front of the medium the materialised form began to arise until there was a full form materialisation before my very eyes.

Q: How long did the process take?

A: About five minutes from nothing to full materialisation.

Q: Do you have a laboratory of some sort now?

A: There is not necessarily a need for a laboratory where I am in the spirit dimension, but I do quite often visit chemists and such that work in laboratory environments on this earth vibration to learn new skills. I must go now. It has been a pleasurable experience to be able to speak to you good people.

Something fell, or was pushed, between my left arm and my wife's right. My wife also said she felt it. Music followed, accompanied by bangs, clashes, rattle-swinging, drum-sticks, and so on, and all without reference to the music, and amid a good deal of reports of touches, interspersed with the occasional mild scream from my wife. Almost everyone appeared to report touches or minor knocks. Immediately the music stopped, one male sitter reported that two rings were over his wrists. Tim asked for the music to be changed: a nice uplifting tune as the energy was becoming a bit thin.

The medium's wife expressed renewed gratitude for her apport. There followed a reprise of 'An Englishman in New York' and a loud farewell from Tim. Then another song, unaccompanied this time.

The music faded out, and the séance ended as the red light was slowly restored amid some heavy breathing. The sound of sealing tape being ripped off the light switch was accompanied by instructions from the circle leader to remain completely quiet while my wife retrieved her camera from the anteroom. The medium's eyes were protected from the flashlight for the four or five pictures taken – these showed the medium strapped to his chair in the centre of the room. When the medium's blindfold, which had been used as a gag, was removed the circle leader drew attention to the remnants of ectoplasm still on the material.

So what is my assessment and what comments on the evening? Well, it is almost an article of faith among many psychical researchers that unless physical phenomena are capable of being clearly witnessed, or alternatively that infrared video recording is available, no persuasive evidence of anything 'paranormal' is possible.

Although the spirit portrayed as Sir William Crookes explained why an infrared video camera might be damaging to the medium at his present stage of development, the general rule of the need for evidence may be broken if the other security measures justify an unambiguous assertion that deception on the part of the medium was impossible.

The nature of the ties would have prevented the medium, no matter how strong or agile, from escaping his bonds without first cutting them. Even had he been able to do so, he could not have regained his seat and retied the knots unaided, employing a new set of uncut ties, unless he had been helped by someone able to work deftly, accurately and swiftly in pitch dark. No one in the séance room could have attempted that without ready detection. Moreover, my careful examination of the chair showed no sign of any movable join.

Finally, the reversal of the medium's cardigan while he was still bound to his seat defies normal explanation. The precautions here were superior even to those employed by Schrenck Notzing on Eva C, who was sewn into a single garment, or on the physical medium Jack Webber, where less sophisticated tying methods and materials were used.

During the brief time when the red light was switched on, we could all see the medium draped with a white cloth-like foam substance, presumably ectoplasm, albeit not with great clarity in some cases. It corresponded in appearance with many of the photographs showing ectoplasmic emissions from past mediums. However, the facilities for overt examination of it contrasted rather strikingly with those available to Harry Edwards in his supervision of Webber, who was extensively photographed by flashlight in various stages of ectoplasmic production, apparently without injury to the medium[2].

For this apparent anomaly, I was given two reasons: Webber may well have been more strongly developed as a medium; the photographs were all taken with the consent of the spirit guardians, who had an opportunity to withdraw the vulnerable animation spirit from the ectoplasm before photographs were taken. There is also the very large number of flashlight photographs taken by, or on behalf of, Schrenck Notzing, and reproduced, albeit poorly, in *The Phenomena of Materialisation*[3].

The voices themselves could not have come from the gagged medium. The only other 'regulars' on whom suspicion might rest were the medium's wife, the circle leader – who was seated next to me, and whose voice and location would have clearly identified him – and the host, who was seated at the opposite end of the room from the medium. Any of these possibilities would have easily and immediately detectable by those present, as well as likely to be defeated by listening to the tape recording. While the communications did not contain anything that could be regarded as convincingly evidential, the information was consistent with what is known of Crookes, and the answers to all questions were unhesitating, coherent and sensible.

To me, the remaining physical phenomena did not appear to be susceptible to any normal explanation, considering that hand-holding (despite Eusapia Palladino's purported skill in hand-substitution) effectively ruled out those closely associated with the

medium: for example, the medium's wife, the circle
leader and the host.

D)FOOTNOTES TO EXPERIMENT 2:

1. 'Substantiate' is used in a strictly accurate, but today unaccustomed, sense here.
2. Jack Webber, who died aged 32 in 1940, was a prominent physical medium, who was befriended by the
   celebrated healer Harry Edwards. He published many photographs showing Webber, without a cabinet,
   and with apparent ectoplasmic emissions from and around him.
3. This was a semi-public séance as distinct from one where regular sitters meet privately in a domestic
   or home circle.
4. It is not unknown for ostensible children to perform quite adult functions in séances. Mrs Osborne
   Leonard's principal control was Feda, whose childish mispronunciation and temperament was allied to
   considerable intelligence, as here.
5. There appears to be a direct relationship between the 'strength' or vitality of the ectoplasm and its distance
   from the medium.
6. The circle leader's nickname.
7. A popular street market in West London.

Contemporary Experiment 3 – Circle A

This third sitting is as reported by John Samson.

In January 2003, I walked into a purpose-built timber
room in the back garden of a house and sat with
approximately 20 other people, nearly all of who were
strangers to me, and awaited events to unfold.

The medium came into the room and was then tied
hand and foot, by strong plastic straps, to a heavy,
padded chair. I was invited to examine these bindings,
which were designed in such a way that they could not
be untied, but released only by cutting them. As an
additional precaution, the medium was also gagged – a
gag which I was also allowed to check. The chair was
positioned in a corner of the room and curtains drawn
round it forming an effective 'cabinet', enclosing the
medium and the chair to which he was tied.

On the floor of the room was a piece of rectangular
wood, on which were placed items such as a conical
trumpet tipped at both ends with luminous paint, a
child's toy drumstick, pencils and sheets of A4 paper.

All lights were extinguished, except for a tiny red one, which was attached to a mini-drive taperecorder placed behind my chair. I had been offered a seat close to the cabinet between the circle leader and another regular member of the circle in charge of the recording. Once the light was out, we were asked to join hands with our neighbours, so that nobody could move their position without being detected.

The séance began with recorded music being played, with which we were asked to sing along. I usually find this part of the proceedings a trifle difficult, since I invariably have never heard of the tunes played. Happily, however, on this occasion, the first piece played was the Pachebel's 'Canon' – one of my favourite pieces of classical music. Following this, and several other musical items, we experienced various kinds of phenomena. After the trumpet had whizzed about the room, describing circles in the air at great speed and tapping me unerringly on the head and shoulders, voices began. To judge from the responses of regular circle members, it was clear that these voices were frequent and familiar visitors from the 'other side'.

The first voice was that of a boy, a regular visitor I understand, with a highly mischievous sense of humour. After an eldritch shriek of laughter, he enquired if any of us were frightened. His function was obviously to be the court–jester for the evening. Other voices followed, accompanied by footfalls that could clearly be heard about the room. A new voice – rough in manner and speech – introduced himself as 'Jack' and I felt my hand being seized by a large, masculine hand, and pumped vigorously in greeting. Shortly after, we heard a child's voice and footsteps moving about. Suddenly, I felt a small hand grasping mine and a young cockney voice – very close and immediately in front of me – said: 'Hello – it's nice to meet you mister.'

A little later, one could hear the rustling of paper from the middle of the room, where the aforementioned items had been left on the flat, rectangular board. Not long after, we heard the scuffling of sheets. Again, I felt a small hand tugging, this time at the collar of my polo-neck sweater and pushing paper down the front of the garment.

The voice of the humorist Peter Cook then presented itself, and we were treated to an abrasive commentary delivered in a typically jocular and facetious manner. On being told that there was another professional show-business person present in the room, he approached me, and then declared himself of the opinion that I seemed 'a bit starchy' to him. This was somewhat malapropos and made my wife hoot with laughter when I told her of it later.

There was also a communication from Sir William Crookes and the brief appearance of Louis Armstrong. Crookes gave me a piece of personal information to prove his identity and said as much before he left the circle. Armstrong simply sang a few bars of music.

After more music, bangs and thumps and the sound of drumsticks, as the séance drew to a close, we all heard a resounding thud from the centre of the room. When the lights went up a little later, there in the centre of the room was the chair, last seen in the 'cabinet', and into which the medium had been tied. And still sitting, motionless in the chair, with eyes shut, was the medium. The plastic ties were undisturbed and securely in place. However, there was one significant difference: the medium's cardigan was now back-to-front. The medium still seemed to be in semi-trance state. However, he was gradually brought round, while we all sat quietly waiting. Once awake, he left the room for a breath of fresh air and the meeting broke up. It was then that I became aware of a drumstick that had been pushed into my hand by a child's fingers during the phenomena.

It was only when I got home and was discussing the evening's events with my wife, that I remembered the paper that had been pushed down the front of my sweater by the child's hand. I pulled out a sheet of A4, folded into quarters. I opened it and saw, written in large, childish handwriting, the words 'Sir A.C. Doyle'. I have been speculating ever since about the significance of this.

Some people question the fact that experiments are carried out in the pitch-black and that regular sitters could be purporting to be 'materialisations'. However, as you can see from the precautions taken and the fact that sitters all hold hands, with guest and independent sitters scattered among regulars in most cases, this cannot be the case. John and Mike Roll (later in the next chapter) each speak of a small child's hand holding their own.

It is easy to dismiss things when you are not there to experience them yourself. However, there is an experiment you can do at home to prove that it is impossible to fake a full materialisation experiment. Go into a blacked-out room, and in order to make sure you really cannot see a thing, also where a blindfold. Have someone personally close to you stand outside the room with a complete stranger. Then ask one of them to enter the blacked-out room.

How long do you think it will be before you know who has come into the room – your friend or the stranger? Bearing in mind that you can speak to the person as soon as they enter the room and touch them. One second? OK, perhaps two seconds, but no longer, even if the stranger was trying to convince you of their disguise. It makes you think, doesn't it?

8

CONTEMPORARY EVIDENCE: FURTHER CASE STUDIES

*'In a time of universal deceit, telling the truth
is a revolutionary act.'*

GEORGE ORWELL

FOR THE PAST 150 years, experiments with materialisation mediums have been able to provide what was
missing from Sir William Crookes's experiments (with
recently deceased people being physically reunited with
friends and relations still on earth).

Ever since the death of the materialisation medium Helen
Duncan in 1956, every scientist reading the subject of
survival after death as a branch of physics has been eagerly
waiting another first-class medium like her to come on the
scene. Alas, while there are many developing at the time of
writing, I do not believe any as yet have reached her
incredible standard. However, as soon as is possible, it will
be essential to repeat the pioneering experiments using the
sophisticated recording equipment that we now have
available to us[1].

Unfortunately, hardly any scientific work was carried out with Helen Duncan, but we do have the report that was submitted by a team of magicians headed by William Goldston, the founder of the Magician's Club. They were astounded when their 'dead' magician friend, The Great Lafayette, materialised and spoke to them. Goldston sent a report to *Psychic News* confirming that Helen Duncan's mediumship was absolutely genuine and that no magician could possibly duplicate the phenomena that he and his fellow magicians had witnessed.

Lorraine, Duncan and Crossley

Of course, many people have been researching, experimenting and sitting for years. Nevertheless, it does seem that mediumship occurring at the moment, although rapidly progressing, is a far cry from sittings in the past: those of the mediumship of Florence Cook, Alec Harris, Jack Webber and Helen Duncan – and more recently that of Rita Lorraine. Her sittings, in my opinion, provide the most remarkable of all the stories of past sitters.

In the 1980, Alan Crossley, author of *The Life of Helen Duncan*, sat with the Leicester-based Rita, her husband Steve, and circle members Pat and Barry Jeffery on seven consecutive nights. He described his experiences in *Psychic News*[2]:'It was one of the most momentous occasions of my life. After 40 years' or so experience in "psychic" matters, particularly physical mediumship, and I have sat with the finest mediums this century, the events ... unfolding at Leicester are not matched by anything I have seen before.'

Alan witnessed a plethora of physical phenomena including direct voice, levitation, apports, and: 'above all, the materialisation of human forms of those who have passed from this earth'. He testified that he saw a beautiful lace dress – worn by Laura Lorraine, Rita Lorraine's grandmother and a regular communicator through the circle – as well as a complete military uniform, worn by Sir Oliver Lodge's son, Raymond.

Crossley was also reunited with his wife, who had passed away four years previously. In addition, he said that one of the main communicators was Helen Duncan herself: 'She reminisced over several incidents that were known only to the two of us ... I heard that familiar voice again ... I knew Helen Duncan well and sat in her séances on several occasions. My book was written primarily to repudiate the persistent slander and gossip which carried on long after she passed.'

After her trial at the Old Bailey in 1944 under the Witchcraft Act, the law was changed in 1951 and replaced with the Fraudulent Mediums Act to enable spiritualists and mediums to practise without the threat of prosecution.

In 1982, *Psychic News* journalist Alan Cleaver visited Rita Lorraine's Leicester circle on many occasions, often at crucial stages in its development. He was also present at one of the first séances when sitters were allowed to see and touch a hand. The séance trumpet – an aluminium cone with a luminous strip at each end – was brightened as much as possible. At first all that could be seen was the silhouette of a hand and what seemed like black lines, then he recalled:

'I saw the hand properly for the first time. The hand was smaller than a human one, probably five inches in length, and looked as smooth as porcelain. It had no nails and no bone joints. It was thinner than a "normal" hand. Perhaps the best description of it is as a hand without the bones. We were shown it moving its fingers wriggling about quite freely. At one point the whole arm appeared. There seemed to be no joints even on the elbow. It was naked.'

Alan was asked if he wanted to touch the hand and told to hold his hand out back upwards. The trumpet came up to his hand to supply the light. 'Then I felt it and the others saw my hand being stroked. The hand felt hot and clammy with an almost sticky quality to it. It stroked me for maybe 40 to 45 seconds. It then stroked Pat and Barry's hands'[3].

On later visits to the circle, Alan witnessed the hands becoming more formed, being able to feel the bones of the hands and the varying size of different ones.

The unions with the Helen Duncan soon became paramount to Rita's sittings, and formed a pinnacle of Alan Cleaver's career. Then, in 1982, he sat in on the exercise of getting Helen Duncan's daughter, Gena Brealey, to witness an experiment – and I think you would agree that there is no way a daughter could be taken in by an impostor impersonating her mother. So, Gena Brealey was invited along to see what she made of it.

She came away fully convinced that the experiment was genuine and that yes, indeed, her deceased mother was returning, fully materialised, and that she had indeed been talking with her for over an hour.

Alan's findings in the 1980s completely vindicated the pioneering repeatable experiments of Sir William Crookes and the Nobel Laureate Professor Charles Richet's under laboratory conditions. Alan, now editor of the *Hampshire Chronicle*, has kindly let me reproduce his original report and findings, which I think compare well to other reports of experimental sittings with Rita which followed.[4]

Alan Cleaver and Rita Lorraine

What constitutes proof of life after death? Is it a series of messages received from a clairvoyant or trance medium? Is it seeing an apparition of someone you know to be dead? Is it making objects paranormally move, appear or disappear – or is it something more? Psychic researchers have argued this point for years and the debate is likely to continue for many years more, but the most convincing evidence I have witnessed was when Gena Brealey spoke for about an hour to her dead mother Helen Duncan through medium Rita Lorraine.

Rita Lorraine, her husband Stephen, and friends Pat and Barry Jeffery, had been sitting for some months developing a link with the dead when one of their regular communicators claimed to be Helen Duncan, the material-isation medium who died in 1956.

As with other communicators, Rita and the other sitters asked for proof. Some of this could be checked out through articles and books already available on Helen, but the opportunity to check some of the more obscure references came when Helen's daughter, Gena Brealey, visited a Spiritualist church in Leicester. Rita and friends invited Gena to tea and, by casually guiding the conversation, were able to check some of the other points made by the spirit entity claiming to be Helen. The data checked out but they did not reveal to Gena that her mother was apparently communicating to them until Rita broke the news to Gena in August 1982, and it was arranged for her to visit the circle.

At the test séance were Gena, Rita, Pat, Barry and myself. Not surprisingly we were all a little nervous, not least Rita the medium. The séance was held in the front room of Pat and Barry's home; as with all séances it was held in complete darkness apart from light supplied by luminous paint on the edge of the table and on some of the musical instruments or objects used during the séances.

We lay our hands on the small table and it began to tilt. The light was turned out and the table continued its gyrations. Some apports (paranormally produced objects) were felt to land on the table and eventually we put the light back on. The apports were several deep red carnations and a single red rose, which had been placed in front of Gena. Gena broke down in tears and cried, 'What greater proof could I have?' She revealed that at her mother's funeral she had placed a single red rose – unknown to other relatives and friends – in her mother's hands in the coffin and whispered, 'I love you.'

Years later, a medium had told her of this (seemingly relaying the message from Helen) and also said that one day her mother would return the red rose to her. Now the rose had returned. The light was extinguished once more and through raps the spirit communicators asked us to put the tambourine on the table. This was heard to rattle vigorously and, thanks to the luminous paint, seen to dance around the room. The tambourine was discarded and the communicators asked for the séance trumpet, a metal cone with luminous paint on the ends through which spirit voices had on many occasions been clearly heard.

Normally, at this stage, the outer circle removed Rita's shoes and watch and threw them on the floor. However, Barry had expressed some concern about Rita's watch possibly being broken by this and asked if they could be more careful. This time the watch was placed in my lap. I estimate that it was dropped from a height of no more than a couple of inches. Rita is sitting perhaps seven or eight feet away and was by this time entering a trance state; the room was pitch black. This was one of hundreds of occasions during my many visits to the Leicester séances that whoever was causing the phenomena clearly demonstrated their ability to see in the dark.

Rita was then in trance. Soon the trumpet was seen, with the help of the luminous strips at the ends, to rise into the air. Helen had always been the first to speak at the séances I had so far attended but that evening Russell Byrne was the first to speak. Russell had died from cancer on 14 August 1963. He was nine years old. For most of the time he communicated as a nine-year-old boy; he said this was for 'identification' purposes. On rare occasions, he spoke as a man.

Speaking through the trumpet he introduced himself and welcomed Gena to the circle. Laura, using the trumpet, sang to the circle, along with the taped music playing softly in the background (a feature of every séance). Laura was another of the regular spirit communicators. Then Helen came and spoke, through the trumpet, to Gena. She spoke first of the rose and declared: 'If I could, I would bring you a thousand roses.' There was a break halfway through the séance but, apart from that, Gena spoke almost continually to her mother for more than an hour.

Much of the conversation was of a highly personal nature and Gena asked me not to release all the details. It contained not only information about Gena's childhood and Helen's work as a medium but also about her family today. It was difficult to follow carefully all the conversation because of the use of unfamiliar Scottish slang and because they spoke about people and events of which I, and the rest of the sitters, had no knowledge. For example, at one point Helen said she had disposed of all the illnesses she had suffered from during her physical life in the 'midden'. Gena explained afterwards that this was Scottish slang for a rubbish tip. Helen also used the term 'poke', saying Gena could take her rose home in a poke. Gena explained afterwards that a poke is a paper cone. Helen also told Gena to take the rose home to her husband, George. This puzzled the rest of us until Gena explained her husband had 'green fingers' and would know how to make a rose bush from the one bud.

Gena, a Spiritualist, cried during the séance and she could scarcely be called an over-emotional person. I was quite convinced she would not be afraid to denounce the voice if it was not her mother. But to make sure, I rang Gena three days after the séance and she reiterated there was no doubt it was her mother. There were no 'difficult' moments during the test séance and the conversation flowed freely and easily.

The Byrnes and Rita Lorraine

Experiments with Rita Lorraine took place in various locations, including the house of Barry and Pat Jeffery, who have themselves been physically reunited with their 'dead' 16-year-old son in the course of hundreds of repeatable experiments. The boy, Michael Jeffery, died in a motorcycle accident. The same thing has happened to Gwen and Alf Byrne, who have been physically reunited with their son Russell on scores of occasions. He had died of cancer at the age of nine. Gwen tells her wonderful story in her book *Russell*, which gives great hope and comfort to grieving parents all over the world.

After conversing with his Mother Gwen, I include Russell's story here of how he was reunited with his parents and the incredible 1980s sittings which happened as a result.

In August 1963, Russell Byrne died of cancer, after being diagnosed a few weeks earlier. After several months had passed, Gwen began looking into the possibility of life after death and researched various clairvoyants. After five years of such investigation, having started from a completely uninformed base, Gwen became convinced that there must be a spirit world and that we carry on living after death.

On 14 August 1982, Gwen was away, and her husband took a call from Alan Cleaver, in his capacity as a reporter for Psychic News. Alan broke the news: 'I have a message from your son – for his Mum'.

At the end of the half-hour conversation, it transpired that on the previous evening he had attended a sitting with Rita Lorraine in Leicester, some 200 miles from the Byrne's home in Essex. Alan, Rita and the sitters had not known the Byrne family and vice versa. It turned out that on the 19th anniversary of his passing, Russell came through at one of Rita's sittings. There, through automatic writing, he had given them the telephone number to call and requested that he wanted to speak with his Mum and Dad. So duly Alan invited the couple to join them at the next sitting.

A week later, seated in the lounge, the trumpet came forward and through it Russell's voice sang the song 'Where is Love' from the musical Oliver!, and a piece of willow was apported onto Gwen's lap, tying in with the line 'Is it underneath the willow tree...' A large willow tree grew in the front garden of the Byrnes' home.

The couple began regular trips to Leicester and the more they sat, the stronger the phenomena became.

Emma Heathcote-James

Soon, they saw energy manifested around the room in the form of small lightening flashes. Amid them could be seen materialised forms, including Russell. They experienced transfigurations and materialisations through energy. In time, these physical forms progressed and became more and more solid. Quoting from Gwen's description of them: 'as solid as you or I'.

Luminous objects were soon placed in the room so the forms could be seen – Russell would often run around the room wearing luminous trainers that everyone could see.

Michael Roll and Rita Lorraine (I)

Someone else who witnessed young Russell was Michael Roll. The sitters taking part were Rita Lorraine, the medium; the hosts Pat and Barry Jeffrey; and Michael himself. During the sitting, the following (Michael refers to them as 'etherians') appeared: Russell Vernon Byrne, who had died of cancer in 1963 aged nine; Helen Duncan: the physical medium; Raymond Lodge, son of the scientist Sir Oliver Lodge (Raymond was killed in WWI); Boyrie, Rita Lorraine's father, who did not speak; Laura Lorraine, Rita Lorraine's grandmother appearing as a young lady with a beautiful operatic voice; James Arthur Findlay, philosopher and historian, who died in 1964; Michael Jeffreys:, the 16-year-old son of Barry and Pat, who had been killed on his motorcycle. This is Michael's testimony:

Barry sat by the locked door alongside a lighted candle. Rita was on the same side of the room in the other corner, sitting in an easy chair. Pat sat opposite Barry.

She operated the tape recorder, which played light opera music, including the Student Prince, quite softly. I was about two yards from Pat. There were a number of other empty chairs around the room. A small wooden table stood in the middle of the room.

Rita signalled she was ready and relaxed in the chair. Barry asked me to be very still while Rita went into trance, but said that once the people from the unseen universe arrived, I could relax and join in the conversation. Barry then put out the candle. All I could see was the luminous drumsticks left in the middle of the room by Barry. After a few minutes, there was a loud bang from Rita's direction. It sounded like her chair had been lifted a few inches and dropped. There was a rapping on the table. The number of raps indicated that Helen was present.

Duncan spoke first: 'Michael, you are very welcome, it is a great privilege to have you with us.' She made some very complimentary remarks about me to assure Barry and Pat that I was perfectly trustworthy and to tell Rita when she awoke. 'I will speak to you later Michael.'

The small table was moved across the room and came to rest very gently against my legs. A young girl's voice said, 'Laura.' A hand gently touched my knee. Then Laura broke into a beautiful song, with great feeling. She was standing only two feet from me. It seemed that she was singing this song especially for me, a newcomer. She took my hand and held it for about 20 seconds. It was undoubtedly the hand of a young lady. Warm and exactly the same feeling as our hands. Bones and finger nails. There was also a delightful smell of hyacinths. After this wonderful welcome the etherians showed me a breathtaking demonstration of physical phenomena. Boyrie, a musical director on earth, showed me the power he could generate with the drumsticks. I was a little apprehensive that the sticks would smash into my face; but as a sign of reassurance Boyrie gently touched my knee.

Raymond Lodge donned a luminous jacket and boots provided by Barry. Then Raymond came over and stood in front of me; a very tall man, over six feet. With one of the drumsticks, he hit his body, arms and legs to show me how solid he was. He walked back and forward, straight through the table. After stamping around the room, he sat down next to me in a wicker chair. As a gesture of assurance he squeezed my hand very tight.

I said I was using the work of his father, Sir Oliver, every day. He answered that he knew that I was. He got up and took off the coat and boots. He threw the boots at my feet, one striking me on the shin. I felt it, but it was not painful. After this awe-inspiring demonstration, Russell brought us down to earth with some first-class clowning. At first I didn't understand why these intellectuals were allowing a nine-year-old to take charge. I was secretly annoyed and very disappointed. Now I understand perfectly. It's a section of the session used to break up a highly-charged atmosphere – this visit from the etherians lasted from 8.45pm to after midnight. Without the light relief and laughter we would all have been emotionally drained.

'Hello Michael,' he said, 'Your name's not Michael, I am going to call you by your real name, Rolly Polly. It sounds a bit clownish and you are not really a clown, but you can sometimes turn yourself into a clown.' All my friends at the golf club call me Rolly Polly at stag nights, when I clown about as I did in my old rugby days. Russell went on: 'I was with you and Rita this afternoon; fancy saying that you thought I was earthbound. I am definitely not earthbound. By the way, I saw the food you ate, one of those funny egg things with sausage around it.'

Helen said it was time to give Rita a break. Rita woke up and had a cup of coffee while we excitedly told her all that had happened. It does seem so unfair that Rita never sees all the wonderful things that happen. The etherians will not even allow a tape recorder. I understand that recording will be allowed but they are not ready yet.

Boyrie took the drumsticks, now freshly dipped in luminous paint. He used paint to show his hands. Laura also showed me her small delicate hands. I could see all the lines. She sang another beautiful love song, moving freely all around the room. After a while, she took hold of my hands, lifted them right up into the air and then down to the ground. Russell clowned with Rita's coffee cup. It sounded like he was pouring it about. The table came over to me. Helen, I think, took my hands and gently pulled me forward, placing my hands on a very wet table. Another firm hand gripped my left arm. I said, 'Who is that?' No answer. Helen then said: 'We have a lovely surprise for you, Michael.'

A voice said something I couldn't understand. Helen called across to Pat in a broad Scottish accent: 'Pat, please turn down the tape.'

I heard someone say, 'James Arthur Findlay here, Michael.' He gripped me very firmly on the left arm. I was still leaning forward. Helen said, 'Now keep very still, Michael.' Arthur Findlay put his other arm around my shoulders and squeezed me tight. Patting me on the back, he said, 'I am right behind you Michael, all the way.' He repeated it and let go of me.

I have been working for years to bring Findlay's work to the attention of the public. Can you begin to imagine how I felt? To diffuse this electric atmosphere Russell came clowning across. 'I have a present for you Rolly Polly.' I could hear something being unwrapped.

I said that it sounded like Christmas. Russell said, 'You should have been here at Christmas; what fun we had! The sack of presents came down from the ceiling.' Russell's small hands took mine and placed a doll in them. With a loud shout, he said, 'It's a clown.'

Helen began a long talk about her plans to bring enlightenment. I said that my only aim was to try and change the way people think and behave throughout the world. If only I could try and change the Irish situation by telling the people how badly they have been let down by the priests. She agreed with me that there are no such things as Christians, Jews, Moslems or any other sects. They were all invented by man for his own selfish aims. She also pointed out that there were no racial differences. In the etheric world everyone is the same.

Helen told us that it suits her mission to keep the old Helen Duncan identity at the moment and said: 'Perhaps one day I could graduate to a higher plane and then I could easily lose my old identity.'

I mention the names of a few famous people who I would like to bring to a session one day. Helen said, 'We do not care who comes here, whether they are kings or dustmen. The only attraction famous people have for us is their ability to tell a lot of people about the truth of survival.' I got the impression that, in spite of the fun, Helen and Raymond's work is far from flippant. There is a very serious purpose to physical mediumship. Nothing less than an attempt to bring enlightenment to mankind and to bring to wider attention the existence of the vast unseen universe that we all graduate to after we have finished our short stay on earth. If only people could be told that they are accountable for every thought and action. What a transformation there would be. There was a another five minute break.

Boyrie then started with the xylophone, sitting next to me. He played perfectly with the music on the tape recorder. When he had finished, Raymond Lodge came and sat in the chair next to me. We talked for about 30 minutes about many subjects. He asked if I had anything I wanted to ask him. Of course, I had ten thousand questions, but I am afraid I was suffering from shock or excitement and my mind had gone blank. Raymond sensed this and started to talk about his large, happy family while I settled down.

The question of flying saucers cropped up. I said I thought they came from one of the million inhabited planets that astronomers estimate to be in our physical Milky Way galaxy. He confirmed that this is correct. This is why they need a vehicle, as etherians do not need transport to move about. He pointed out that, obviously, the people from other planets are much more advanced than us. This is why they do not make contact, as we are still not well-developed enough to receive them. We would probably shoot them. Next time I will ask how they are able to travel faster then the speed of light.

I asked on behalf of my millions of fellow sportsmen if sport is played. Raymond confirmed that every sport was played with great enthusiasm – all those that do not involve killing animals. I pressed him on my favourite, cricket. I thought his answer was charming and also very exciting. He had obviously sensed my deep love of cricket and said that it is played in a different way in the etheric world. It is conducted without animosity, rather like it used to be played on village greens. He said, 'However, I will not go deeply into this, Michael, as it will spoil the wonderful enjoyment of finding out when your time comes to join us.'

As the conversation continuted, Raymond said, 'Just a moment – somebody is approaching the house.'

A key went into the front door and a relation of Barry and Pat's, whose house we were in, went down the hall to the kitchen. It showed that the etherians have thought of lookouts as part of their organisation. Raymond, like Russell, also referred to the private conversation I had with Rita during the afternoon. He reminded us that it was Foxes (the sisters in America), who first gave the clue to the unseen universe. Rita and I had talked about the plates on the wall with foxes. Raymond then got up from the chair and walked away.

Russell quickly came on the scene and said, 'Rolly

Polly, we play golf here but some golfers call it "gof". They knew they were in heaven because they leave the "l" (ell) out.'

Russell then said, very sincerely, that he is going to come home with me down the motorway to make sure that I got home safely. A number of very interesting things happened on that journey that only he and I would know about. I am certain he will tell me the details the next time we meet. Helen then said it had been a wonderful night and that I should bring my mother the next time I come. She said my mother is a very wonderful woman who has had a hard life. She would be very welcome in the group. Helen then said, 'We must close now,' then suddenly, 'No, we still have more time.'

Laura then came to me and sang another beautiful love song, holding my hands most of the time, sometimes stroking the backs of my hands. She also kept throwing her dress over my head and pulling it away so that my hair was pulled forward. All the time there again the smell of hyacinths. I have never experienced such a feeling before in my life, one of overwhelming love.

At the end of the song Helen said goodnight and Pat said goodnight to her son Michael. He answered his mother with great affection, explaining that he did not take part this evening as he had been asked to stay in the background because it was to be a special night for Michael Roll. He then came across to me and said how welcome I was in his house. He said, 'You know, Michael, this is the best house in the world, it's so full of love.' I thanked him very much for allowing me in. I was overcome and couldn't say any more. On this dramatic note of love, the etherians departed.

Rita came round from her trance and Barry lit the candle. I did not really recover for 48 hours. If this experience has such a shattering effect on me, a person who has read psychic science all my life, what must it be like for an outsider? I could not even eat any of the lovely food that Barry and Pat offered me. As if all this was not enough, when Rita was driving me home to her house in another part of Leicester, the car cassette switched itself on. 'Oh, that's Russell, he's always doing that,' she said. I borrowed the tape of Chopin that was inside her stereo and played it all the way home to Bristol.

I reflected for some time on the sitting before recording my final thoughts. The first thing I noted was I had not been nervous once during the experience, because I have spent 30 years reading the subject.

I thought the physical phenomena demonstration was not done as a cabaret act. Raymond Lodge showed me that he could take a physical object, a drumstick, striking it hard on the physical table with loud bangs. Then, by altering the consistency of the physical atoms of the table, he pushed the drumstick through the table. It did not go effortlessly through and I have thought hard for an analogy. It was like a sharp knife going through soft polystyrene.

When Raymond was wearing the boots and coat, he also walked back and forwards through the table. Again the physical boots passed through the physical table.

The consistency of the atoms must have been altered. I cannot wait to show my nuclear physicist colleagues. I took it that Raymond was able to alter the consistency of physical atoms by using his mind. I felt I let my scientific colleagues down by not being more scientific with my questions. I will rectify this if I am kindly invited again. However, I would not be surprised if the etherians refused to answer certain questions. Maybe we are not sufficiently advanced to be allowed to receive the answers to every question.

When Raymond stood in front of me, striking himself all over with the physical drumstick, he opened his coat and thrust the stick into his heart. This time the stick did pass effortlessly through – the knife and polystyrene effect.

The other wonderful thing that happened was the fact that I fell desperately in love with Laura. The same sort of 'teenage love feeling' or the William Holden and Jennifer Jones type of love in the film Love is a Many Splendoured Thing. Again, this was done to me for a purpose not just for fun. I am aged 45 and, until now, have been scathing about this type of love, insisting that it is purely sexual infatuation, specifically designed for our physical universe to perpetuate the species. This experience made nonsense of this dogma. I have since found out that all the other men who have been to the circle have also had this wonderful feeling.

Apart from my clown there were many other objects round the room that have appeared at previous meetings. The etherians insist that they come from our physical universe and that they will not be missed. What a fascinating subject for the scientists.

Michael Roll and Rita Lorraine (II)

Michael went back for a second visit on 9 April, 1983, and was allowed to feel the materialised Laura's shoes, feet and ankle.

She sat next to me on the settee and showed how she could gently pin my hands by stepping on them. Her shoes felt like dancing shoes.

Helen took a physical drumstick and used it to materialise yards of material which covered the floor of the room. All the sitters were allowed to feel it. Unlike the circumstances around an apport, when the interval came the floor was clear of any material. This material was from the etheric world and not of our physical world. The etherians say that apports, like my clown, come from our physical world.

The etherians proved to me that they can use physical objects, change tape recorders, etc. I then asked the vital question about nuclear war. Could they make the buttons inoperable? Raymond answered this by saying it was not his responsibility. This type of decision, which involves the destruction of the planet, must rest with God. By 'God', Raymond meant the unknown power in the universe that creates galaxies and puts life onto planets. Decisions of this magnitude are not for Raymond Lodge or anybody else.

There seems to be a definite hierarchy based on character. The etherians who are organising this vital communication with us come from the plane of existence to which the vast majority of people on earth graduate. When we leave our physical bodies, we are not suddenly given the secrets of the universe. Those who are prepared to make the effort to gain knowledge, and do the right thing, will progress to more advanced planes of existence. Helen, Raymond and Russell have perfected the art of speaking to us over a period of two years. They cannot just make any Tom, Dick or Harry appear and speak when the fancy takes either them or us.

This time, with great difficulty, they did manage to bring my father, who died of cancer in 1967. He embraced and kissed my mother and I. He spoke very softly and I did not recognise his voice. However, I knew without any doubt that it was my father, because I smelt him. He was completely overcome with emotion. As Helen led him away, I heard her say consoling words like, 'Now this is only your first time, perhaps in the future.'

A question was asked about atmospheric conditions: did it affect the communication? Helen said it makes no difference except that a thunderstorm overhead would not be very good because it would affect the magnetism. 'That's one for you, Michael, and your scientific friends.'

I carried on the conversation with Raymond Lodge about flying saucers, asking how they can travel faster than the speed of light. He replied, 'The advanced civilisations that visit your planet have learnt how to dematerialise matter. They have to travel in a vehicle because they have not learnt to transport themselves independently like we do in the etheric world. They are very advanced but not as advanced as we are. You need never worry about their intentions because they are good people and would never hurt the inhabitants of earth.'

There was also a question about pets – what happens when they die? Helen replied that if a dog is walking along a street and it is run over by a bus, its etheric body carries on down the street and returns to its home. It carries on with all its usual familiar things. It never suffers any sense of shock and for an animal that has a love bond with its owners there is no sense of separation for the animal. Pets are always reunited with people that showed them affection in due course. This includes any pet, goldfish, birds, and any living creature. Love is the bond. Love seems to be stronger than the atomic glue in the nucleus of an atom, and as any nuclear physicist will confirm, this is very strong indeed.

When a physical object is passed through another physical object by the etherians, my analogy of a knife through soft polystyrene was shown not to be correct at all times. The etherians are able to alter the consistency of atoms at their ease. This time they demonstrated this by showing me how they pass the physical drumstick through the physical table with the knife-and-polystyrene effect, then again without this effect. The second time, the drumstick passed effortlessly through.

I asked about a particular Bristol cancer clinic that offered alternative therapy and treatments. Raymond

Lodge said they were correct to work together with the surgeons and more orthodox medicine. In some cases, a cancer can be cured by will power or tremendous concentration. Imagine the cancer as a large cauliflower and start to break it down into thousands of pieces. This sometimes has the effect of destroying the cancer. I understand this method is already being taught at the clinic. the etherians we are in contact with do not know the cure for cancer any more than we do. Why should they?

It was also very interesting that Raymond Lodge did not seem to know very much about acupuncture; in fact he called it 'aquapuncture'. He said that if a patient has complete faith in the acupuncturist, it is wonderful what can be accomplished. I reminded him that major surgery can be carried out under acupuncture anaesthesia and that it worked on animals. This proves it is nothing to do with faith. He did not seem to have an answer for this. He mentioned something about nerve systems in the body and that the orthodox doctors do not recognise acupuncture only because they are prejudiced against it.

Again, I was so pleased that Raymond made these elementary mistakes. It proves to me that just because somebody is in the etheric world, it does not mean that they are automatically an expert on every subject. These people are exactly the same as us, but now they are living in the universe that is made up of atoms that are much finer then our physical atoms.

Martin Masters was scathing about some remark that Brother John made in the Psychic News. Brother John said it was possible for a carpenter to carry on with his profession in the etheric world. 'What rubbish', Masters said, 'just as if we on earth could destroy trees in the etheric world.' Raymond answered that maybe Brother John did not explain himself very well. Carpenters can certainly carry on with their work. The wood materialises; there is no question of destroying any trees.

I asked if the etherians would be able to communicate with one of our world's leading scientists if he accepted my invitation to attend. They answered that they could, but no answers will be given if it is considered that we have not advanced sufficiently to receive the knowledge: 'But surely your colleague as a scientist would be very interested to see and speak to us anyway.'

I asked if the etherians could clear up once and for all the question of reincarnation. They answered that, no, they could not. They do not know any more about reincarnation than we do. Raymond said: 'Who am I to tell little Russell that it's his time to return to earth. If there is such a thing again it must come from a higher authority.' This certainly made sense to me. I said who in their right mind would want to leave your wonderful world and come back to earth?

'Exactly,' replied Raymond Lodge.

I asked Helen why she could not arrange to materialise in daylight as had been the case with her sessions on earth. She answered that I had been misinformed, because all her meetings took place in the dark. She also said that this new method is much improved because they have now done away with ectoplasm. They were trying very hard to improve the method of communication all the time. It was the old 'heavy' ectoplasm that killed Helen in 1956. Ever since then, etheric scientists have been working flat out to refine the chemistry. There must be an ectoplasmic covering but it's now so fine we can no longer feel it covering the bodies of the etheric people.

Michael Roll's accounts remain among the most detailed and fascinating records of such sittings with Rita Lorraine, who has continued with psychic research and anomalous phenomena, though she no longer practises as a physical medium.

Everything now rests on another fully developed materialisation medium coming forward and letting scientists of the calibre of Archie Roy complete their experiments. However, this poses the problem mentioned earlier; the number of fully developed physical mediums able to create materialisation at the present time can be counted on one hand, together with the number of those still developing. However, as soon as one develops to the extent of the likes of Rita Lorraine, to be able to produce full materialisations in red light and allow sitters night vision goggles every time, then it will be all systems go.

George Cranley and Alec Harris

As discussed elsewhere in the book, the mediumship of Alec Harris was second to none. He passed over on 12 February, 1974. George Cranley, a sitter and now president of the Noah's Ark Society, had met Harris through a friend of his mother while on a visit to Cape Town. She invited him to

sit in on a materialisation circle in 1963. This is the way
George reports it[5]:

As a regular sitter in Alec Harris' circle, my mother's
friend told me that on one occasion her husband
materialised in his Royal Marines uniform, walked out of
the cabinet, kissed her and called her by a pet name not
known even to their children. Naturally, I was very
excited at the prospect of a sitting, particularly as I had
read many dramatic accounts of Harris' mediumship in
Two Worlds and Psychic News. One Friday morning I
received a telegram which simply said 'Séance
tomorrow night. Can you come?'

I wired back that I was on my way, went down to the
airport at Cape Town with my whole month's wages,
bought a ticket and flew to Johannesburg. I arrived
three hours later and stayed in a hotel overnight. Next
day my friend took me along to a modest house where
I was introduced to the medium, Alec Harris, and his
wife Louie.

A small bedroom, part of which had been curtained
off to provide a cabinet, was used as the séance room.
There were eight of us, four in the front row and
four immediately behind. I was invited to sit next to
the medium's wife, directly in front of the opening in
the curtains.

Louie led the singing, which went on for about 20
minutes. I was beginning to get a bit restless when, all
of a sudden, I heard a voice from behind the curtain.
'That's Alec's guide, Christopher,' said Louie. 'He speaks
with a lisp.'

The curtains parted as if drawn by unseen hands and there stood what looked to be a vague outline next to the medium. There was more singing before the curtains opened again to reveal a more fully-formed figure, but one still not clear enough as far as I was concerned. 'That's Alec's mother' said Louie. 'She comes quite often now that Alec is getting older'.

The room was lit by a number of red bulbs. No dimmer switches were used, which made it very easy to distinguish everything quite clearly. After more singing, there appeared from the side, not the front, of the curtains, an American Indian. He stood in front of my friend. 'Greetings Black Feather,' she said. He was her guide and materialised whenever she was present. After exchanging a few words he turned towards me and said, 'Will the young man from Cape Town come forward?'

Before the séance, Louis told us not to touch the materialisations unless invited to do so, as it could harm the medium. I stood up and walked over to the figure. He was bare from the waist upwards, with one black feather in a band round the back of his head; the lower half of his body was draped in ectoplasm. 'Feel my skin', said the figure. He was very tall, well over six feet. I had to stretch up to touch the side of his face. Copper-coloured, the skin had a leathery feel about it. Then he said: 'Feel my chest.'

I did as requested and noted the chest was quite solid. 'Hit me on the chest,' he said.

'Are you sure?' I asked.

'Yes,' he replied, and I did so.

'Harder,' he said. Using the palm of my hand, I hit him on the chest.

He never flinched and again said 'Harder!' Summoning all the energy I could muster, I hit him on the chest. My hand just bounced off. The figure turned to me with a half-smile on his face and said, 'You may sit down now.' I did as he suggested, absolutely staggered. How did he do it? Was there a trap door on the floor, was it Alec Harris on stilts? As the figure walked back behind the curtains, they parted in the front and a young woman came out and stood in front of me holding a little baby in her arms. One of the sitters recognised her and explained, afterwards, that she had died while giving birth. Both mother and baby had passed together.

During the course of the séance, which lasted around three hours, about 14 people materialised. One I found particularly interesting was a figure which appeared in half shadow and draped in ectoplasm. Only half the face was visible; he didn't speak. I heard crying behind me. One of the ladies asked, 'Is that you, Uncle Arthur?' The figure just nodded. After the séance, I was told that Uncle Arthur had died from a particularly nasty type of cancer. Half his face was eaten away so he was unable to speak before he died.

Every circle seems to have a child guide whose job it is to lighten the proceedings when things became too emotional. This was no exception. A little cockney boy named Ginger materialised and said to me: 'Feel my nose.' I bent down to touch his nose, which felt as though it had been squashed. 'I was hit by a tomato,' he said, 'in a can!' This was followed by peals of laughter, which immediately lightened the tension in the room. Ginger then walked round greeting all the sitters, returned to the cabinet and disappeared. As he walked, I noticed a trail of ectoplasm behind him, which flowed under the curtains and back towards the medium.

The most fascinating part for me was when a guide dressed in the most beautiful white robes walked out of the cabinet and said: 'The young man from Cape Town, come forward.' I did and, literally, found myself looking straight into his eyes. I asked who he was. 'I am one of your guides,' came the reply. He told me his name and the area where he came from, I asked if I might touch his robes, but he said, 'Please don't, but I will show you something.'

He then fully extended his arms so I could see the whole of the spirit drapery. Neither his face nor neck was covered with any sort of ectoplasm. I stood there thinking:'How can I touch you?'

So I said, 'May I touch your hands?' He said 'Yes,' and held them out. I took them in mine and thought to myself:'Now I've got hold of you I'm not going to let you go until I've got to the bottom of this.' I was determined that whoever this was, he wasn't going to get away from me! We chatted for 10 to15 minutes about my future spiritual work. Much of what he said seemed impossible at the time, but a lot has been fulfilled.

Suddenly he said, 'I have to go now.' So, I thanked him for coming but still held onto his hands. Something made me look down at his feet. As I did so I saw the bottom half of his body dissolving away, but his hands were still solid. Then his hands melted away between my fingers, yet my hands were still closed. The last thing I saw was his head slowly sinking to the floor saying 'I am going now,' disappearing under the curtains like a streak of light.

At the very end of the séance, the curtains parted. Christopher said: 'We have no more power left.' As he spoke, from the medium's solar plexus, came two great clouds of ectoplasm to the left and to the right. In the ectoplasm appeared, literally, hundreds of miniature faces. The guide said these were some of the people who had been present but unable to get through.

What was very noticeable during the séance was the earthy smell unlike anything I had smelt before or, indeed, since. I wouldn't describe it as pleasant, but I had a headache for about three days afterwards. Louie described it as the power that had been drawn from the sitters.

The above are all descriptions of sittings that took place in the past, albeit fairly recent past. Contemporary circles are also producing interesting work. As before, the evidence from such circles – of both established and developed mediums – requires me to keep them anonymous, for obvious reasons. Once more, I will ascribe them letters of the alphabet in order to make the necessary distinction and identification.

Three More Contemporary Experiments
Contemporary Experiment 4 – Circle D

The following is a report from Ron Gilkes who attended an experiment with this particular circle[6]

Jenny, my deceased daughter, first spoke about four years ago and was very tearful and saddened about passing to spirit by her own hand. I don't know how I was able to compose myself when I recognised Jenny's voice saying, 'Hello Daddy; I am sorry Daddy.' I can only presume it was strength given to me by others.

Since then, Jenny has communicated several times during séances held at seminars given by the NAS (Noah's Ark Society). I have converted a barn on my property and called it Jenny's Sanctuary. Here, afternoons of clairvoyance have been held and used for circles which have been started. Furthermore, I have had the privilege of hosting the NAS on several occasions. At the first séance, Jenny communicated and spoke for nearly ten minutes. She also wrote a note for me and held my hand briefly. When she spoke with George Cranley, the NAS President, he suggested that she could try walking across and giving me a kiss.

By September 1999, I had suffered the loss of my father and problems with Jenny's mother. Moreover, the Sanctuary was virtually demolished when a runaway army truck ran into it. This turned out to be a blessing, as the insurance compensation has allowed me to construct a far superior replacement.

Chris, a friend of mine, contacted me to suggest a sitting with a medium, 'D'. Naturally, I jumped at the chance. I travelled with Chris to a venue called the Spirit Lodge. After a short prayer by the dozen or so people there, the proceedings began. Many of those who were present received communications from friends and relatives. During the séance, Dolly (one of the medium's guides) began to speak to us and was just about to introduce another communicator, when Jenny, virtually pushing her way through, made herself known.

Dolly spoke to her saying, 'Well, come along dear, you've done this before,' and I could hear Jenny's voice saying, albeit softly, 'Daddy.' I knew that it was her. However, when I replied, I did not say anything that would diminish the evidential value of the communication. Jenny commented on my concern about her mother but added that I should not worry. She continued to speak, giving an unmistakable, evidential quality to her communication. She also referred to her grandfather, saying that he was fine, although he had been very confused when he first passed over. She recalled the occasion when she met him and this cheered him up. Jenny then made reference to her nanny and asked that her love be passed on to her.

She told me that she now had a new pony. She added that she also had Janey, the one I had bought for her some years earlier. She then mentioned how she was teaching her granddad to ride! Jenny commented on the building work in respect of the new sanctuary and said how she looked forward to its completion. She told me that one of the builders was very interested in the subject of survival and mediumship, and when I asked her to which of the builders she was referring, she told me it was the young one who has 'a lovely sense of humour'.

At this point, the proceedings came to the most wonderful part for me. Jenny said 'Daddy, if you sit very still, can I come and give you a kiss?' I replied that I would do as she had asked. We then heard her making her way across the room; as she did this, there was a loud noise as she knocked the microphone (or part of her ectoplasmic self draped across it). I could hear her moving towards me and wondering if my glasses would get in her way. I asked whether she wanted me to remove them, but she said no and clasped my fingers and pulled my hand up. I could feel her mouth against my hand very clearly and everyone heard her kiss. At this point she said, 'I love you daddy'.

After making her way back across the séance room she said 'Daddy, when it's [the sanctuary building] all finished, will you put a rainbow in the window?' I said that I would and she concluded her visit by saying: 'Goodbye daddy.' I said goodbye to her and she left after saying that her granddad might speak to me on the next occasion.

Contemporary Experiment 5– Circle D

The following is a report is from Nick McGlynn, who joined in with another experiment at a different time with Circle D[7].

[My wife] Marie passed over one morning in hospital. She had suffered from emphysema, heart failure, kidney failure and dementia. That same evening, the medium was due to hold a direct voice séance. I phoned and asked if I could attend the meeting as there was nowhere else I would rather be than with like-minded people. He agreed immediately and I asked him not to tell anyone what had happened that morning or anything about me He did not want to create an emotional atmosphere, but rather a happy and harmonious state for the séance. Naturally, I hoped that my wife had arrived safely and was free of pain.

After the communal singing to raise the energy and vibrations, Frances, better known as Judy Garland, sang 'Over the Rainbow', after which she came to me, held my hand, and said, 'This one is for you, honey.'

To the group she said, 'Halfway through the next song, another person will take over – something that is very difficult but we'll try it.' Then she sang 'Maria' from West Side Story. Halfway through, Dolly – a female impersonator when on earth and a regular communicator – took over and finished the song. Just hearing this song was enough, as no-one there, not even the medium, knew my wife's name. With a thankful heart, I relaxed and felt my Marie was OK now; but the best was yet to come.

After Dolly had joked a little and answered a few queries he told everyone he was missing the big celebrations going on behind the scenes. Then he added: 'Now we are going to try and do something that has rarely been done before and that is to bring someone through whose energies and vibrations are not fully over our side, which makes it difficult and very dangerous for the medium. So, I must ask everybody to be perfectly still, or as still as possible, and, where you can, join hands, except Nick.'

With pounding heart, I thought, 'Will she, won't she, can she? What's going to happen?' and began to hyperventilate. As I managed to control myself I heard Dolly say, 'Come along, I'm going to help her through because the person is not completely stable on our side yet, and it's very dangerous for the medium.' Gently, he coaxed her and after about ten seconds a fairly weak voice said, 'Nick, Nick I'm home, I'm home,' (in the special way I used to announce my arrival to her when I came home).

I said, 'Oh Marie, how wonderful. I'm so happy, so happy for you.'

She replied, 'Thank you for being with me last night [in the hospital]. I'm glad all the trouble and all the pain is over for you. They have been so kind to help me to come'.

'It's marvellous and lovely of everybody, I'm so happy,' I said.

Dolly was heard saying to her, 'Walk into it, all you have to do is walk into it [the ectoplasm].'

I said, 'Keep calm, take your time, I'm here. Thank you for touching me and holding my hand, isn't it wonderful?'

She replied: 'I love you, I'll wait for you.'

'Have you met your Mum and Dad?'

'Yes, also Leslie.'

'Leslie?'

'Yes, with a large gin and tonic.' Everyone exploded with laughter as Marie became stronger.

I said, 'I'm so happy you are free of all your pains. The doctors were so good with you.'

'Yes. I want you to have a ball,' said Marie. Go out and have a good time.'

Light-heartedly, I said, 'Right! I'll spend all your money, sell all your jewellery and go to Switzerland and see Anil [the couple's close friend] in Australia.'

Practically screaming, Marie said, 'Yes! Yes! The money is no good to you here. I am fine but a little weak. I just could not believe it when they said I could come back tonight.'

'I'm really amazed,' I said.

Marie said, 'It's a terrible strain on him [the medium], I haven't got everything over yet – it's hard for them to do this.'

I responded, 'They were very good and kind to do it.'

'Have you decided when you'll stick me in the box?'.

'I'll sort you out, just me, Jaycee and Ravi. I'll get rid of you quick as you are in Spirit, not here.'

'Yes, that's right. I don't want to be hanging around. Be with you. Be with you on the day of the cremation.'

'I understand that, love. We love each other.'

'I'll wait for you. Apparently I'm getting a house here and I'm allowed to choose the bloody wallpaper.' Laughter erupted, as I was always the one who chose what went on the walls!

'Don't forget to tell the children [our four sons],' she said. 'I didn't like the song they sang ["Maria"] in the beginning. I've always hated it.' There was more laughter. She kissed me on the cheek and stroked my hands through it all, even digging on the arm when I said that I would sell all her jewellery and spend the money!

Marie said, 'I must go now, it's dangerous for the medium.'

I replied, 'I love you and hope you will come again another time.'

'Yes. Goodbye, darling,' she said.

Contemporary Experiment 6 – Circle B

In Norfolk, on 15 May, 2003, a select group of sitters experienced physical phenomena through the mediumship of Circle B. Although the medium had retired from giving séances outside his Home Circle some years earlier, he has done a limited number at specially chosen venues. This is Alf Winchester's account[1]:

The sitting began in the normal manner, with circle guides and helpers talking through the entranced medium, while, behind the scenes, spirit operatives were preparing for the physical phenomena.

One of the sitters was invited to sit beside the medium and was thrilled and amazed to witness the passage of matter through matter. The medium's arm was passed through a plastic electrical tie, which attached him to the chair arm. Walter Stinson, the spirit operative who orchestrated this phenomenon said that he 'made no apologies' for doing this particular demonstration at each séance where there were new sitters present.

He said, 'Many would call it a miracle, but it was nothing of the kind, it merely showed that anything is possible when the right conditions exist between our worlds.' I was also privileged to witness this phenomenon some years ago, when in good red light I saw the medium's arm passed through the ropes tying him to the chair arm, with a loud noise like a whip being cracked.

The next phenomenon to occur was the perennial favourite of sitters – airborne trumpets. To a rousing musical accompaniment, the trumpets, three at one point, performed complex aerobatic manoeuvres in time to the music. Some sitters had trumpets accurately placed on their heads and hands showing complete spatial awareness on the part of the spirit controllers.

Walter Stinson invited a sitter to sit in front of a specially-constructed table, which had a glass top that was underlit with a red light, the intensity of which could be varied by means of a rheostat. From the direction of the medium (still secured to his chair), a lump of ectoplasmic matter was seen to move onto the table. Through the entranced medium, Walter said that he was going to materialise his hand. Almost like someone placing a hand in a glove, a large right hand, with quite thick fingers, was seen to emerge from the matter. The fingers were manipulated before retracing back into the lump of matter.

Walter asked for the sitter to place her hand on the table with her fingers at the centre. The hand again materialised and touched and slapped the hand of the sitter. He then asked the sitter to feel his fingers and nails and invited her to confirm that she was feeling a perfectly normal hand with the feel of a normal live human hand. This she was delighted to confirm. The sitter returned to her place in the circle and Walter asked for the table to be removed. The curtains on the cabinet containing the medium were closed and the medium, apparently awake at this time, said that he could see a light in the cabinet.

The curtains parted and a faint orb of diffused light was seen to dart from the cabinet and then return. After a few rehearsals, the light became a little brighter and Walter, in materialised form, left the cabinet carrying the orb in his right hand, displaying it around the sitters and showing the silhouette of his fingers, hand and forearm against the flow from the orb that he held.

During his walkabout, Walter spoke to us in a loud, clear voice, identical to the familiar drawl that we hear when he speaks through the vocal chords of the entranced medium.

From the cabinet, Walter said that a visitor, who was known to several of the sitters, was going to attempt to materialise. The cabinet curtains flew open and a person's footsteps could be heard walking from the cabinet, saying excitedly, 'It's Alan, it's Alan,' in the unmistakable tones and mannerisms of Alan Crossley. He went around the circle and approached and greeted enthusiastically only those persons whom he knew. He came to me talking exuberantly, in a frail-sounding but loud voice, grabbed my head and shook it wildly, and then took my hands and vigorously shook them between his.

Before returning to the cabinet, he explained that he had sat in a materialisation circles on numerous occasions (he wrote a book about his sittings with Helen Duncan), but he never thought that he would have the opportunity to be the one who materialised and was amazed and delighted to be able to do so. The uniqueness of this event occurred to me. Alan Crossley was a former President of the Noah's Ark Society and here he was materialised and touching me, another former NAS President, and all made possible through the mediumship of another former NAS President, Stewart Alexander. This was a truly extraordinary meeting and for me the highlight of a truly wonderful evening spent with our spirit friends.

The whole séance lasted for 135 minutes and I have only reported the most important happenings. During the séance a number of sitters were evidentially reunited with their loved ones. Towards the end of the sitting, Walter said, 'We try to balance phenomena with communication from loved ones. My aim is to complete the work that I started when I worked through the mediumship of my Sis ("Marjory", aka Mina Crandon) so many years ago. What you have seen tonight, folks, is only the beginning.'

All the sitters agreed that they had experienced a truly uplifting evening of communication between our two worlds. Personally, I can't wait to see what the spirits have in store for us.

9

Scientific Proof: The Etheric World Discovered?

'All recent scientific discoveries are tending more and more to show us that the universe includes un-sensed forces, which in turn operate on un-sensed substance, and that the universe is infinitely greater than our physical senses can comprehend.'

Arthur Findlay *The Unfolding Universe*

IT WAS IN ARTHUR Findlay's first book, *On the Edge of the Etheric*, that he explained how we all survive the death of our physical bodies, making it clear that proof will eventually come from within the atom. Just over half a century on, I consider his claims to have been validated.

I think we need to look at our vocabulary, which is often insufficient for describing phenomena. It is all well and good to use the word 'believe', but I prefer to accept some things, reject others and, after much thought, place anything that I am not too sure about in my pending tray for further thought and enquiry.

Believing and Knowing
Carl Jung was once asked, in a live interview in the 1960s,

if he believed in God. After a pause, he replied that it wasn't a case of believing, but of 'knowing'.

It is a revealing observation. Each of us in our lives develop a belief in *something* For instance, as a little girl I believed in the tooth fairy and in Father Christmas. It is only now, with experience, investigation and hindsight that I can say that I was mistaken. My beliefs were wrong and had I been misled. Although Father Christmas, the tooth fairy and such ideas enriched my childhood and excited my mind, I now *know* that the tooth fairy was really my over-generous parents; that my stocking was delivered to the foot of my bed on Christmas Eve by my father (who also ate the mince pie and sherry, leaving a few crumbs and a thank-you note!). I now *know* that Mr Right wasn't at all right; and that knights in shining armour who bound to your rescue usually have their own agendas – and most are not necessarily the most savoury of characters.

In essence, as much as we want to believe, we must bear in mind that there is a difference between 'belief' and the actual 'knowledge' of its existence. When researching, it is important not to reject evidence simply because it may conflict with your own cherished beliefs. We are products of our environment and upbringing. From the time we are born, we absorb information from our family, friends, schools and the media. Inevitably, beliefs become deeply emotional; but they are also neurological. We know that when we have any information not consistent with our own beliefs – be it on ghosts, UFOs, politics or anything – we tend to reject that information. Why? Simply because our mind will put up the defences necessary to protect our bias, to bolster our partiality. It does this because the inconsistent information will cause us anxiety, elicit fear and will destabilise us emotionally.

Nowadays, science often overrides personal belief. One can still believe in the tooth fairy, but no one has actual knowledge or experimental proof of it. If they did, that information would override the belief, and the tooth fairy would become 'scientific knowledge'. This is an important point to grasp because what ultimately is important for you to know and fully understand on this planet earth is the truth based on information that can be repeatedly tested for validity. The 'scientific' evidence for the afterlife is irrefutable and has never been shown to be wrong.

What is Scientific Proof?

Over 2,500 years ago, the ancient Greek scientist Pythagoras was the first to propose the idea that the world was round. However, without the necessary and full mathematical support for such an idea, it was 300 years before this was accepted, when another Greek scientist, Eratosthenes, presented a mathematical theory for a round Earth. The minimal mathematics that Pythagoras and Eratosthenes used were fine for their time, but the basic idea lacked the impact it should have had because they were unable to provide complete proof; they had the idea and the basic formulae, but no experimental proof. This only came much later when the Portuguese navigator Magellan and his crew completed the first circumnavigation of the world in 1522. The 'flat Earth' adherents were completely destroyed by a combination of experiment and existing mathematical theory. Scientific proof must consist of repeatable experiments backed up with a theory that has a mathematical base.

Proving survival after death presents exactly the same challenge. However, it is not quite as easy, because we are dealing here with phenomena that are beyond the range of our five physical senses. In order to detect this type of phenomena, the seemingly invisible, we have to work with a medium – a 'machine' that can do the job.

There are precedents, however, for identifying what couldn't be seen. It was the invention of the achromatic microscope in 1830 by Joseph Jackson Lister, with its vastly increased range of vision, that enabled his son to write his paper on antiseptic surgery.

From that moment, we had the proof that reality also exists in the invisible. Radio and television receivers also detect 'invisible' phenomena. They are mediums detecting signals at different wavelengths and frequencies. By analogy, this is why we are forced to work with a human physical medium in order to prove survival after death, as no machine so far invented is as sophisticated as the human mind and brain.

However, great care is essential when carrying out experiments using people, as there can be no room for error where lives are concerned. This type of mediumship is very draining for the medium and requires the use of carefully-planned environments and conditions.

Survival After Death – Early Experimental Proof

What do being in love and having a headache have in common? The fact that neither sensation can be produced in a laboratory to assess whether or not they empirically exist.

So, if neither can be duplicated, does it mean that love and pain do not exist? Of course not! It is just that such things cannot be induced – just like spontaneous, one-off ADC visions or messages. Nevertheless, according to some sceptics, if any phenomenon cannot be tested in the laboratory, then it cannot exist. Even there, they are wrong! The afterlife *has* been accessed, assessed and tested in laboratory setting.

What I found quite astonishing was the fact we have actually had the experimental proof of survival after death since Sir William Crookes published the results of his experiments in the *Quarterly Journal of Science*, the leading scientific journal of his day, in 1874. This research consisted of repeatable experiments, under laboratory conditions, with Florence Cook, a materialisation medium. International teams of scientists, including the Nobel Laureate for Medical Science, Professor Charles Richet (French team), Professor Von Schrenck Notzing (German team), Dr Glen Hamilton (Canadian team) and Dr WJ Crawford (Irish team) have all since repeated the experiments that Crookes began. With physical mediums, they have produced full materialisations and obtained the same results – that people who had once lived came back and proved they had conquered death and – etherically – were still very much alive. So why were such results not headlines back at the beginning of the 20th century?

These experiments lacked the backing of any detailed mathematical theory. Post-Crookes experiments, in 1929, Sir Oliver Lodge said, 'We have to be guided by the facts, and if the facts seem incredible, as they do, we have first of all to assure ourselves that they are facts, and then conclude that there is a department of knowledge to which we have as yet not got the key.'

Now, as we begin the new millennia, over 130 years later, we now do have the key, the missing mathematical theory, to back up these revolutionary experiments.

Materialisation Experiments – the New Evidence

First, though, to recall the point that 'nothing happened yesterday in the laws of physics that does not happen today'. All those who have more recently taken part in scientific experiments with materialisation mediums are in a position of advantage over the work and conclusions of the pioneers in the field, who had no knowledge of subatomic physics. They understandably thought that something supernatural had taken place. Now that we are armed with the mathematics and knowledge of quantum mechanics, it is important to repeat the pioneering experiments.

The mediums are also improving. Crookes had just one etheric person to work with and she had 'died' so much earlier that they were unable to get any relations to take part in his experiments. Now, this part of the scientific exercise has now been carried out very successfully. For example, the Jeffery family have been reunited with their 'dead' 16-year-old son in over 300 experiments. The Byrne family have been reunited with their nine-year-old son, who 'died' of cancer, in something like 100 repeatable experiments.

It is asking a lot for a medium to work with scientists to prove survival after death, because they have to put their lives in the hands of those who carry out the experiments. Nevertheless, Gwen Byrne has now published a book of the experiences and it is providing tremendous comfort to all mothers and fathers who have gone through the ordeal of losing a child. So where are the journalists and broadcasters waiting to interview these families and to share their wonderful experience with every person in the world?

A New Spiritual Era?

Predictions and prophesises have filled every era and every culture, signals heralding the end of civilisation. One in particular suggested that there would be signs to watch for: the first would be a return of the Jews to their ancient homeland, the second a huge and escalating level of violence, the third would be 'wars and rumours of wars' and the fourth that there would be a rapid increase in the number of earthquakes. This last point was dealt with in an article by Michael W Mandeville entitled 'The Chandler Wobble' (in *Nexus*, Vol 9, No 5, June–July 2002, pp 49–54.) This showed a graph of earthquake events of magnitude greater than 2.5 on the Richter scale. In 1973 there were 4,500, in 1990 these had more than doubled to 10,300 and by 1998 there were 17,000 such events, an increase of 7,000.

The final sign would be a revelation as to the true nature of the world – what it all meant. This has formed the basis of much work by Ronald Pearson and it is this that we will look at next in more detail.

10

THE EVIDENCE IS HERE:
THE RONALD PEARSON
REVELATIONS

*'One of my guiding principles, also, has been the scientist's motto
"Take nobody's word for it" ("nullius in verba"), a corollary of which is
that if scientists as a whole denounce an idea this should not necessarily be
taken as proof that the said idea is absurd: rather, one should examine
carefully the alleged grounds for such opinions and judge how well these
stand up to detailed scrutiny.'*

PROFESSOR BRIAN JOSEPHSON

FEW WILL DISAGREE that research into etheric substance is the most important scientific task in history.
Michael Roll, founder of the Campaign for Philosophical
Freedom, admitted to 'jumping the gun and getting
overexcited' when he saw a report in the *Sunday Times* on 13
December, 1981, indicating that physicists could have been
wrong for 40 years about the make-up of the Universe. They
were saying that nine-tenths of the Universe is 'missing'.

When we look through a telescope at a galaxy, we are
only seeing one-tenth of the mass that ought to be there.
The motion of distant galaxies and the stars in them can
only be accounted for under the laws of gravity if there is
far more mass associated with each galaxy than there is in
the visible stars that comprise the galaxy.

One theory for this missing mass centred around a ghostlike subatomic particle called the neutrino, first identified in 1956. The neutrino showed that there was something in science that behaved like a so called ghost by moving effortlessly through solid matter. The report said a neutrino would stand a good chance of penetrating a thickness of lead stretching to the nearest star without hitting anything. Such luminaries as Arthur Koestler reacted to this news (in his book *The Roots of Coincidence*) by saying that science had finally discovered something in the building blocks of nature that started to give a rational explanation accounting for the millions of reports from people who say they have seen a 'ghost' walk through a solid wall. Etheric people are made up of finer subatomic particles than we are.

However, despite Michael Roll's reaction, his astrophysicist friends Mike Scott and Sam Nicholls, although very supportive of the afterlife survival theory, did not share his enthusiasm that the neutrino was the missing piece needed to make up the etheric universe. So, the hunt continued. In stepped Ronald Pearson.

Establishing the Truth

Ronald Pearson was born in 1925, the son of an extremely enigmatic schoolmaster who became deputy headteacher of Chesterfield's William Rhodes School and was well-known for his hands-on approach to science and the way he built apparatus for experiments for use by his students. Young Ronald soon showed a grasp of science and mechanics and would help his father in his workshop at home. At school, he developed an interest in mathematics and the physical sciences going onto serve an apprenticeship at a local engineering company. During the apprenticeship, he studied at Chesterfield College and graduated with an honours degree in mechanical engineering[1].

While the development and invention of the jet engine by Sir Frank Whittle was making headlines, Pearson was busy inventing a new kind of engine of his own – the gas wave turbine, which he developed to demonstration stage and which resulted in his appointment as a research officer at the National Gas Turbine Establishment.

In 1955, aged just 30, Pearson accepted a post as lecturer in mechanical engineering under Professor Horlock at Liverpool University. He remained there for five years before a move to Bath University, where he lectured in thermodynamics and fluid mechanics for almost 20 years. It was only following his retirements in 1986 that he switched his attention to physics and cosmology. It was through his study of cosmology and ether physics that he came to accept survival after death as a reality.

In so doing, it seems that Pearson provided all the missing pieces for Sir Oliver Lodge's 1933 article, 'The Mode of Future Existence', which was inspired by the work of Sir William Crookes. It had been Crookes' experiments with a medium that produced photographs purporting to show 'dead' people, most famously Katie King, who physically materialised in the laboratory in repeatable experiments. However, we know that Crookes lacked any mathematical theory to support his experiments and that this resulted in his claims being largely dismissed.

In Crookes' day, the ether was thought to be the background medium of the Universe, something which filled all space and which transmitted electromagnetic waves. However, by using modern quantum physics to re-examine Einstein's theory of relativity, Ronald Pearson believes that he has found the mathematical solution to explain the existence of the 'ether'. In a nutshell, he has produced the theory of an all-pervading, intelligent background medium that exists throughout the Universe. In order to differentiate it from the original concept of 'ether' (which is meant to be a structureless substance) Pearson calls it 'i-ther', though I will continue to refer to it here as ether.

He also found that mind had to be part of the structure of the background medium, and it therefore had the potential to be immortal. In other words, his theory and findings posit 'mind' and 'brain' as being two separate entities. When the physical body (including the brain) dies, then the mind (which some may call the soul, spirit or personality) continues as the seat of consciousness, rendered immortal because it is part of the all-pervading intelligent matter of the 'i-ther'.

Ronald Pearson has been working on this for the last 15 years. What has emerged from his research is a picture totally different from that painted by the established physicists. They say that an almost infinite number of universes must have created themselves accidentally. Each has different laws of physics, so that – by chance – just one emerged, so finely tuned that life could evolve. This is the Universe we observe, since we could not exist in any other. Overall, this is called the Anthropic Principle.

In contrast, the solution emerging from Ronald Pearson's investigation is that a basic, overall level of reality exists, having a structure similar to the neural networks of our brains. This seems to have the potential to evolve intelligence. Furthermore, it is a veritable powerhouse, producing waves of energy everywhere.

It seems that this background intelligence so organises the waves, its vibrations, that the matter of our Universe becomes evident. The matter that we observe is not true reality at all, but now appears as a deliberately contrived reality that is more in the nature of the virtual realities we view on computer screens. True reality lies in the invisible.

The Time of Trauma

Many people fear that a time of great trauma may well be approaching, so that we need to do something to ease the pain. Many people accept that parallel universes exist to which our minds attune just as readily as they do to Earth-matter. They believe (or perhaps I should say 'know') that when we depart this life, we re-emerge without destruction into a new environment. It seems that we are privileged to have this insight, because most people on Earth do not. It is therefore important that our knowledge be communicated as widely and as quickly as possible – and this is where we make our connection. The most convincing proof available is given by materialisation mediumship. Surely, it is about time to take more heed of its existence?

Ronald Pearson had discovered what we will call the unseen and normally un-sensed universe. His papers have been peer-refereed and published by physicists in Russia and the USA. It can be argued that Ronald Pearson's work provides the closest answer to such fundamental questions. I say this because it appears to be the only theory that matches materialisation experiments that are the very core of this book's content. His theory explains all ADC experiences and, in turn, can go on to explain logically such things as ghost sightings and most other so-termed 'paranormal' phenomena, which might be better named 'supernormal'.

Professor Richard Feynman, the US Nobel Laureate for Physics who died in 1988, made a statement that I consider to be the axis of this chapter – and indeed this book: 'If your mathematical theory does not match the experiment, then it is wrong'.

However, also worthy of note is the fact that some everyday phenomena fly in the face of all attempts to encompass them in theories. According to the accepted laws of physics, it should be aerodynamically impossible for a bumblebee to fly... and yet it does, oblivious to the fact that formulae say that it shouldn't.

Examining the Pearson Claim

Firstly, one must remember that just because there are flaws in previously accepted scientific explanations of the Universe, this does not *automatically* make Ronald Pearson's theory correct. Nevertheless, I believe his to be the theory that best explains there is an ether/afterlife, though there is no substantiated proof yet.

The basis is one of simple speculation and hypothesis, in that we are taking on face value the fact that the paranormal exist. If we can prove that the ether exists, then Ronald Pearson's theory will be proven and will eliminate the long-held ideas of Einstein and others. Many of life's mysteries would cease to be.

At the time of writing, it seems that only materialisation phenomena and physical mediumship are the best ways to demonstrate, experimentally and in laboratory conditions, that the ether exists. Along with ether are associated phenomena, such as ADC and vision, ESP, teleportation, psychic writing, telepathy, synchronicity, NDE and OBE.

Crookes, along with the international teams of scientists (Richet *et al*), proved survival after death. Now, Ronald Pearson believes he can now provide the mathematical theory to back up the experiments that offer us this proof of survival (which will be explored in greater depth in the final chapter of this book).

Michael Roll is convinced that Ronald Pearson's claims are true: 'When the theory is published and then proved by a series of experiments, Ronald Pearson will go down in history as the greatest scientist since Sir Isaac Newton.'

So, why isn't Pearson recognised this way today? His theory is complex; it takes a lot of time and concentration to follow through. There have also been rumours of the suppression of his discoveries. And his work is undeniably controversial. For one thing, if correct, he proves that parts of Einstein's theory of relativity are seriously flawed.

On closer inspection, this turns out not to be so far from the general direction in which science is now headed. Conventional research attempts to find a 'theory of everything', the idea of the ultimate basis of everything being merely energy splurges or squiggles and almost certainly multi-dimensional. This may be the link between the seemingly irreconcilable massive and tiny quantum forces (with our familiar 'local' Newtonian world somewhere 'in-between').

In so many ways, this is parallel to – and maybe even inspired by – Pearson's work, despite the fact that his background and qualifications are in mechanical engineering. In this research field-hopping he is not unique, following in the footsteps of the eminent researcher Paul Dirac.

Born in Bristol in 1902, Dirac obtained an engineering degree at Bristol University in 1921, after which he began work in the new field of quantum mechanics as soon as it was introduced to science by Heisenberg in 1928. Quite independently, Dirac produced a mathematical equivalent of Heisenberg's work, which consisted essentially of a non-commutative algebra for calculating atomic properties. His subsequent series of papers on the subject, published mainly in the Proceedings of the Royal Society, led to his relativistic theory of the electron (1928) and the theory of holes (1930). Here was someone qualified simply as an engineer who was acknowledged as a leading world figure in the field of subatomic physics and quantum mechanics.

Relatively Speaking

With the benefit of hindsight, some conclude that a scientific disaster took place when Sir Isaac Newton's model of the universe was discarded and replaced by Einstein's theory of relativity. Indeed, Einstein himself said on his 70th birthday, 'Now you think I am looking at my life's work with calm satisfaction. However, there is not a single concept of which I am convinced that it will stand firm. I am not sure if I was on the right track after all.'

If only our contemporary physicists had shared Einstein's scepticism, then we would not have wasted so much time and money trying to match up concepts of quantum mechanics with the theories of relativity. Even Einstein supporter and globally-successful author Professor Stephen Hawking from Cambridge University admits that they are incompatible theories. Yet, other than some Russian scientists and a few 'heretics' in the West, it seems that the whole of orthodox science is locked into a potentially false and outdated theory.

As we have seen, Einstein's theory of relativity cannot explain the outcome of experiments where those who once lived have come back and proved they are still alive. Yet, Ronald Pearson's theory of the ether (his 'i-ther') most certainly does provide a solution, showing ether to have a complex structure, intelligence and consciousness as core ingredients.

Linking the subject of survival after death with the scientific discipline of subatomic physics, as Pearson did, really does seem to present a scientific case for survival after death. Both Pearson and Roll claim that such work will, with the necessary funding, be able to: '...enlighten the world to the truth'.

It is a truth they both know to exist and which has been denied to people for years.

11

THE BIRTH OF SURVIVAL PHYSICS

*'One of the greatest pains to human nature
is the pain of a new idea.'*

WALTER BAGEHOT

RONALD PEARSON'S WORK points towards understanding what might be called the physics of survival.
It provides a grand unification of materialistic science with
phenomena outside its compass. Psychic phenomena and
the survival of death are then *real* phenomena. It's a contrast
with existing, established physics.

Because this new approach began as an attempt to solve
some problems in physics that had nothing to do with the
'paranormal', the inclusion of such matters appeared
naturally as a byproduct of the research. Yet, they turned
out to be the most important features, even though they are
not only ignored, but also strenuously denied by scientists
across all disciplines.

Survival physics came about as Ronald Pearson realised

that a different approach was needed in any work to challenge the accepted view and relate this to the otherwise 'unexplained'. His own mathematically-based discipline seemed to offer the necessary assistance.

His solution recognises the existence of an invisible background medium extending throughout space and interconnecting everything in the universe – something which that had been postulated even before Newton's time: the 'ether'. Unfortunately, as we know, all efforts made during the 19th century to detect the ether had failed. Then Einstein came up with theories of relativity that were inconsistent with the existence of any kind of background medium. Consequently, the idea of any ether existing at all became discredited – until Pearson started his work

Struggling with Contradictions

In order to understand how Pearson's work can explain 'psychic' phenomena we must first look at his theory of how the Universe began and how this challenges the established ideas of such origins.

The 'Big Bang' theory, which states that the Universe was created from a massive explosion, contains some major flaws and inconsistencies. The biggest of these is something called the cosmological constant, a mathematical figure that arose from the failure to explain how this initial explosion would have stopped. It predicts an expansion of the Universe that is many billions of times too great. The theorists couldn't explain why the Big Bang isn't still banging today.

In further speculations regarding the future fate of the Universe, that it keeps on expanding at a decelerating rate or falls back to a big crunch, cosmologists simply ignore this false prediction. Then there is the evidence that some stars seem to be older than the age of the Universe itself. The Big Bang has been estimated to have taken place around 12 billion years ago and some stars seem to be much older. Something is clearly not quite right. Then, in 1998, astronomers claimed to have found that the acceleration of the universe is actually speeding up – and so postulated that so-called 'dark energy' was the cause.

In the light of these and other flaws, Pearson, with his background as a university lecturer in thermodynamics and fluid mechanics, decided that a new theory was needed. At the heart of the original theory was one of the biggest dilemmas facing physicists today – that of how to reconcile the mathematics of quantum physics with those of relativity. This is what Pearson sought to conquer.

Quantum theory is essentially about the movement of things on the extremely small atomic scale. Things at this size seem to move in random and indeterminate ways. Relativity on the other hand is Einstein's theory for how things move on any larger scale. On this scale, objects move in a much more predictable manner – an example being planets orbiting the Sun.

For over 80 years, mathematicians have assumed that Einstein's theory was always right because nearly all subsequent observations have matched his theories. So in that time, they have all attempted to redefine quantum theory so that it could include relativity and, especially, general relativity (Einstein's theory of gravity). So far, they haven't been successful.

Ronald Pearson accepted the mathematics within

quantum theory and revisited Einstein's work. Pearson felt that if his theory could also match the same observational data that had seemed to confirm Einstein's theories, then his own theory could also be valid. In addition, if it also contained no flaws or inconsistencies, then it could even become a better theory. Interestingly enough Ron found that Einstein's well known formula of $E=mc^2$ could be derived from Newtonian Mechanics without reference to relativity, but it now showed that matter was really made out of energy. In Pearson's theory, this is exactly what happens.

The Pearson Theory: A Summary

Ronald Pearson went back to the physics of Sir Isaac Newton and applied to the problem what he called conceptual logic. His resulting theory matched all of relativity's observational data and was free of internal flaws. In order to do this, he had to be highly controversial and dismiss relativity altogether. Thereby, there was no curved space-time. Instead, he said, real quantum waves, expanding from matter, produce density variations of the ether that have the same effects. Furthermore, he concluded, there was no constant speed of light[1].

The Pearson theory of creation thus begins with two forms of energy – called positive and negative primaries. These he likens to the *yin* and the *yang* found in Chinese Taoist philosophy. As posited in theories prior to the Big Bang, these primaries are created from a zero-state of energy. Negative energy, although not widely known, was not new, having been first proposed by Paul Dirac. It was discarded as a theory quite quickly, possibly because such speculation, that space consisted of electrons in negative energy states, was not acceptable.

Pearson found that negative mass and energy are needed – indeed required – to permit the Universe to arise in such a way as to eliminate the problem of the cosmological constant discussed above. The secret of the success in his new theory is found in the way these two opposite energies collide with each other.

When pairs of primaries collide, the laws of mechanics predicted that each partner would, in general, gain energy of its own kind. There is nothing strange about the behaviour of negative energies. If all matter were made of negative energy, then the negative effects would cancel out and it would behave in a way identical to positive energy. We cannot be sure which kind applies. However, it is the mixing of the two kinds of primary that causes the new, strange effects to arise.

For centuries it has been accepted that 'energy can neither be created nor destroyed'. When positive and negative energies coexist, however, this has to be revised to 'energy can only be created or destroyed in equal and opposite amounts'. Both creation and annihilation are now permitted, but another law of motion has to be applied to find which possibility is selected under the conditions being studied. This is the need to conserve momentum (the product of the mass of an object multiplied by its velocity).

In order to understand this, imagine two billiard balls colliding off-centre. We all know that the two balls move off in a predictable sideways and diagonal manner. When ordinary billiard balls collide, the momentum of each –

measured in the original directions of motion –is drastically changed and there is no overall change in energy.

However, this does not occur when one of the primaries carries negative momentum. When the same angle of collision occurs, the two balls move off in the same sideways direction! When these balls of opposite energy collide, neither can alter their momentum as measured in the original directions. But scattering collisions add extra transverse momentum in such a way that they balance. This means that each partner will gain momentum of its own kind and this cannot occur without associated increases of energy. This energy appears from nothing! Pearson calls this a 'breeding' of the energies.

Both velocity and momentum can be represented on a diagram by 'vectors'. These are lines of a length proportional to speed, or mass multiplied by speed, and drawn in the direction of motion of the object being represented, as shown in Figure 1.

As a consequence of repeated collisions, energy is sometimes annihilated, but overall there is a net increase. This continues and levels increase until a critical density level is reached. It is at this point that annihilation can also occur and a solid filament of energy is produced where the primaries are in the process of mutual annihilation. These are surrounded by regions where energies are still being created by collision breeding.

Annihilation does not totally cancel the creation, so a tiny net creation remains everywhere in space. It is this that explains the continuing expansion of the Universe at an ever-accelerating rate. New galaxies need to be created

THE COLLISION OF POSITIVE AND NEGATIVE PRIMARIES

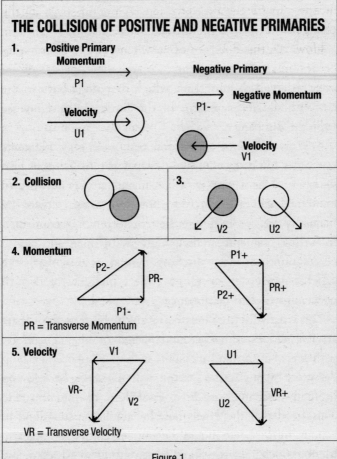

Figure 1.

1. Positive and negative primaries travel towards each other off centre.
2. Collision occurs.
3. Both primaries move off to the same side. A sideways momentum has been added from nothing.
4. Positive and negative momentum are both conserved and the additional transverse momentum (PR+ plus PR−) balance each other out.
5. The opposing directions of the transverse momentum (PR− plus PR+) require associated transverse velocities (VR− plus VR+) to be added in the same sideways direction.

in order to fill the ever-growing regions of space all the time. With this as the basis for calculating expansion, Pearson has estimated a more exact age of the Universe to be around 100 billion years —enough time for the oldest stars observed to form, time which they don't have in the conventional measurement of the birth of the Universe from the Big Bang.

All this breeding and production of energy filaments continues to produce a three-dimensional, filamentous grid structure. This is similar to the human neural network of brain cells. Energy can now travel in waves down the filaments that are, in turn, either connected or unconnected to further filaments at their ends. With open and closed connections, a vast switching system results that, like supercomputers, develops the characteristics of consciousness and intelligence.

This is actually what Pearson means by his term the 'i-ther', an *intelligent* form of background medium or ether. Therefore, with such background mediums such as a 'solid ether' long dismissed by physicists, Pearson, with his strong background in fluid mechanics made a great leap of intuition. He considered that the ether must behave like a superfluid in vapour form – like liquid helium, exhibiting completely frictionless characteristics and so permitting unrestricted flow through the grid of the filaments. It is a concept that now allows the past observational data to coexist comfortably with his new theory. It seems logical, therefore, that from this point in my account to cease reference to 'ether' and to use his term i-ther for this concept.

The waves generated by the action of the filaments move through the fluid as well as along the filaments and are identified as 'quantum waves' of the i-ther. These are then used to produce particles of matter. Pearson envisaged that these interacting waves produce spikes of intense energy rather like interacting ripples on a pond create spikes of water. These spikes of energy create the impression of matter particles like electrons. These would occur in a sequence in time, but not always in the same location. Once particles have been created, the conventional physics of today could then go on to explain the rest of creation – all of the stars and the planets in the Universe.

The waves that produce matter also produce long-range gradients that make the i-ther seem more compressed when near large objects. Negative pressures follow these same gradients and produce a buoyancy type of force on any matter. This is the mechanism of the gravitational force according to the 'quantum wave theory of gravity'. This effect exactly matches the observational data used to previously prove Einstein's theory of relativity. Now they can also prove Pearson's theories, which also do away with the cosmological constant.

His next prediction showed how the initial explosion would shut off to leave a gently accelerating expansion of the universe that matches observation. Flow patterns on a minute scale would appear at some stage, causing the formation of a honeycomb-like set of breeding cells. In each cell the breeding effect push primaries of both kinds towards a central point. Here primaries arrive equally from all directions, so forming the conditions favouring mutual annihilation. Positive and negative primaries vanish to nothing and form permanent filaments. The annihilation cancels nearly all the creation going on in the outer annuli of each cell, and in this way produce a solution for the problem of the cosmological constant. The primary object of the study had succeeded. The spin-off from Pearson's findings is the truly mind-boggling predictions of survival physics.

What It Means

As described, the filaments seem to join up spontaneously to produce, by a form of evolution, a kind of neural network. Consequently, a brain-like structure has arisen throughout space. It has developed a conscious intelligence but can only express itself in the form of organised waves. These are the quantum waves on which quantum theory depends, but they are also the 'vibes' that psychics claim to be picking up.

These waves organise the matter of our universe and those of parallel universes existing in the same dimensions as our own. Worked out in detail, the conscious background intelligence can explain – as *real* effects – all the phenomena hitherto called 'paranormal' or 'psychic'. In other words, everything such as prediction, psychokinisis, telepathy, mediumship, healing at a distance, OBE, and lastly – but most importantly – survival of consciousness after death, with its associated ADC and materialisation mediumship.

These particles or waves of matter have specific frequencies and only appear real to us if on our own particular frequency. With several possible frequencies of quantum wave, several matter systems could all arise from the same underlying grid. All of these matter systems are illusory constructs made up by the i-ther. The system we live in just seems real to us, as human sense organs are developed to respond only to that system. With all this creation of matter, the net result is a positive balance of energies within matter itself – the stars and the planets – and these are surrounded by halos of net negative energy.

With this basic understanding of Ronald Pearson's amazing work, we can now go on to explain subjects like survival after death. As subjects of matter ourselves, we experience the world around us as a being real. However, as matter is composed mainly of space, what we see as real is actually just the illusion of matter created by the filamentous grid and the i-ther at that particular frequency. Our minds are not a function of the brain; they are isolated regions of the i-ther itself, the seat of consciousness.

Perceptual barriers have evolved in our heads to stop us being harmed by the incredible computing power and knowledge of the i-ther. However when we die, we dispense with our matter system and our minds, which in Ron's theory are completely separate from our brains. We live on within the i-ther and interact with some new construct of matter system at a different frequency. This would explain all the evidence found showing that we survive after death.

In the same way, the i-ther and its three-dimensional filamentous grid can also explain how healers really can heal people. It would appear that a healer has less of a perceptual barrier in their heads and can communicate more directly with the Universal consciousness. As the i-ther constructs matter, and as it has huge computational power and memory, it could easily be programmed to reconstruct a person's matter system in a more effective and healthy manner. Healers may also obtain help in doing this by working alongside people on different matter systems and at different wavelengths. Together, their ability to tap into the programming power of the grid, and the underlying i-ther, could enable a person to become a new and better matter system, so healing them.

This effect could occur over long distance. The Pearson theory has already shown that via the fluid alone it might be possible to communicate at speeds of many thousands of times the accepted constant speed of light. That means the speed of propagation of information is no longer limited, as in relativity, by the speed of light. Indeed, it can travel instantly along the filaments. When two people are able to lower and focus their perceptual grid barriers, telepathy could be the result. The better people are at lowering their inhibitory barriers, the more 'psychic' they are and the more efficient they become.

Concepts such as 'mind over matter' – effects such as the bending of spoons without physical effort – can also be explained with the theory. As the grid creates matter as an illusion, tapping into the grid by lowering our barriers should allow us to recreate this illusion. Nevertheless, to us, like everything else, this then appears to be real!

Carrying On
As with all good theorists, Ron Pearson has devised eight experiments that can be undertaken that will prove or disprove his theory. The cheapest of these costs around £15,000, or up to US $30,000. Other experiments involve proecedures that can only be carried out in space. It is now only a matter of time before the world will know if he is right.

To be a true scientist is to be truth seeker. Unfortunately, positions of power and the fear of peer review often close the minds that once were previously open. In the years that Pearson has been trying to promulgate his theories and open them up for discussion and publication he has witnessed all aspects of such closed attitudes. Finding no one who seemed daring enough to publish his papers in the UK, he has had to address scientific audience in Europe and Russia. There, after much struggle he managed to have three publications in Russia (1991, 1993, 1994) after assessment by the Russian Academy of Sciences[2,3 & 4].

Finally, a peer-reviewed article was published in the West in 1977 under the title, *Consciousness as a Sub-Quantum Phenomenon*[5]. Here, his theories were given time and print and it was here that at last he received great accolades for them.

Whatever else, after all the evidence, it is now up to you to draw your own conclusions.

AFTERWORD

'We have it in our power to build the world anew.'

THOMAS PAINE

IS THE WORLD yet ready for materialisation phenomena to be fully accepted? Certainly, I do not think there will ever be sufficient scientific or any other evidence for some of those who never want to accept the evidence for the afterlife. Nevertheless, we all have to die and there are those intelligent enough to take time out to investigate the convincing afterlife evidence. They will find that many of the most intelligent people who walked the planet earth used their scientific knowledge to assess and to accept the afterlife evidence.

So, after asking what happens after death, and after exploring what the next world comprises, what have I learned from it all?

Well, it is not the existence of the continuation of the spirit

– the etheric body – but rather the need to get away from the comparatively trivial question of whether or not there is life after death, and replace it by investigations that can bring us a better understanding of how we should live this life.

If anything at all can be taken from the science described and the findings reported in this book, it is the understanding that – at a deep level – everything is interconnected. All is one. For me, in as many questions that it all raised, it also seemed to answer many others and filled in gaps in my thinking.

From time to time, teachings and philosophies have been communicated by advanced spirit beings. These have dealt with the purpose of life and the human destiny, based on the revelation that we survive earthly death and lead an active life in spirit dimensions. The realisation that one lives on actively beyond the grave alters the conception of life so profoundly that it gives rise to an entirely new religious outlook – one that is diametrically opposed to many of the fundamental ideas of traditional religion. It seems to me that only Spiritualism and Buddhism really comes close, along with more general spiritual ways of thinking.

I do not know if this is the 'truth'. However, as a scientific parallel to the above, I also consider that it is in the most recent developments in the search for an afterlife, and in Ronald Pearson's theory, that the most coherent case yet is put forward for the existence of an afterlife. In turn, I also conclude that this answers so many more questions, making sense of experiences of ADC, sightings of ghostly apparitions, healing, the aura, NDE, OBE and so forth.

Research into such assertions as 'There is definitely an afterlife' or 'There is definitely a God', would be expensive and take a great deal of time. So, this book is the tip of a very large iceberg. I am serving merely as a voice piece for the people inside these pages and ensuring, in part, that their experiences, findings and associated phenomena are placed into the public arena.

Materialisations offer the greatest challenge so far to establishment science, the churches and other academic bodies throughout the world. It challenges them because materialisation establishes once and for all the existence and relative ease of spirit communication with those on earth. Having said that, considering the mountains of 'metaphysical', 'paranormal' and 'unexplained' material available, collating and integrating all the undoubted evidence would be a monumental task.

Yet, if such a thoroughly comprehensive book or documentary series ever came about, it would be a prodigious event. It could – surely, it would – bring about a conscious shift of perception about life in general. It would be sure to shake the sacred beliefs of religion, as well as science, down to their very foundations. Is there anyone out there who will take such a risk?

I wish I had a crystal ball in which I could see 50 or 100 years into the future. I wonder if materialisation phenomenon, and indeed genuine mediumship, will by then be taken as self-evident – just as the radio, telephone, television, space travel and the world not being flat are as now accepted as fact?

I will leave you to decide, and close with the words of the great philosopher Arthur Schopenhauer: 'Any unexplained phenomena passes through three stages before the reality of it is accepted. During the first stage it is considered laughable. During the second stage, it is adamantly opposed. Finally, during the third stage, it is accepted as self-evident.'

GLOSSARY

'We should not go for complete scepticism,
but for degrees of probability.'

BERTRAND RUSSELL

WHEN I FIRST SET out exploring the realms of so-called psychic phenomena and of what has been termed the paranormal, I realised that the topic comes complete with its own extensive esoteric terms of reference. To the uninitiated, much of the terminology seems totally confusing. Consequently, when explaining the content of this book and its underlying theories to family and friends, I soon found that some words were ambiguous and that there was a need to approach the subject from scratch, adopting secular terminology so that it becomes accessible to everyone.

Vocabulary can become complex when explaining the subjects covered in this book. Many words come complete with their own connotations and stigmas. In order to try and simplify this area, I have complied this Glossary – a list of the words that I have chosen to use and the meanings that I ascribe *personally* to them solely in the context of this book. Scanning this alone goes a little way to explain my thinking and acts as a guide when reading the book.

After Death Communication (**ADC**) – A term first coined by Bill and Judy Guggenheim (see Preface) to describe spontaneous (non-induced) visions, apparitions, feelings or messages from deceased loved ones. An ADC is a direct spiritual experience where no intermediary or third party (such as a 'psychic', medium, meditation or a hypnotist) is involved. It is an experience whereby it's claimed that the deceased relative or friend contacts the living person directly and spontaneously on a one-to-one basis. The experiencer not only sees the dead but may also hear, feel and sometimes even smell them. Sometimes, information is conveyed through vivid dreams, but most of the time it comes while the recipient is awake. Often, it is information that the experiencer did not previously know and could not otherwise have known.

Apparitions – See **Ghosts**

Apports / Asports – During physical sittings, some things or objects can appear (**apport**) or disappear (**asport**), that is, they are transported through time and space to a location where their presence cannot be explained by logic. Commonly, 'apports' occur during Spiritualist séances. Stones, gems, items of jewellery, coins, flowers, books, exotic fruits, animals, ancient relics, and even people have been known to be apported into séance rooms, as if from nowhere. Sometimes the apported object remains with the sitters, sometimes it is dematerialised back to where it came from. Many sceptics attribute such phenomena to trickery and believe the objects apported are produced by the medium. However there have been many instances of apports that would require the skills of a professional magician to construct. For example, one medium, Charles Bailey (1870–1947) was able to apport live birds complete with nest and eggs. Apparently, Bailey also was able to apport live fish and even human remains (eg, a skull). Certain Indian mystics are reportedly able to produce *vibuti* or holy ash from the tips of their fingers. They claim it is apported from the next world through their mediumship.

Asports are the opposite of apports. In other words, objects disappear from their location in the material world and may – or may not – reappear. Asports are sometimes explained away as the result of faulty memory – though this fails to account for the reappearance of missing objects in locations where they could not, by normal means, have found themselves. Some argue that we have all experienced apports and asports without recognising them as such – for example, losing something we were certain was in a specific place, only to discover it elsehwere days later without a truly satisfactory explanation of how it got there.

Astral Travel (Lucid Dreams) – Some people have dreams in which they know that they are dreaming, these as known as 'lucid dreams'. They have a dream body, but can will where they go, and to some extent control their experience. Such dreams are very like out of body experiences, the main difference being that one is entered from the dreaming state, the other from the waking. In esoteric literature, travelling in lucid dreams or in out of the body experiences is known as 'astral travel', and the body in which this happens is called the 'astral body' or 'subtle body'. For many people this terminology is obscure and off-putting, hence my reference to it as the 'etheric body'.

Aura – The electrical energy fields that emanates from the human body and from inanimate objects. Seemingly, the human aura can now be photographed and experts claim to be able to predict a person's state of health when analysing such photographs or experiencing (using techniques such as Reiki or other forms of healing) the person's aura.

Big Bang Theory – In respect of the revered Big Bang explanation for the creation of the universe, I consider that one must remember that this is, in the main, a theory, and nothing more. According to it, there can be no such thing as ether. Of course, this is somewhat problematic when looking at so-called 'paranormal' activities. According to Einstein, and orthodox scientific teaching, 'when you're dead, you are dead', and there is no such thing as an afterlife. This would mean that experiences such as ADC and NDE/OBE are just weird brain hallucinations and that accounts of ESP and precognition can be put down merely to odd coincidence. However, research into these areas concludes, more and more frequently, that the existence of ether – or at least of other explanations, dimensions, and so on, is and are distinctly plausible. In turn, one could interpret this as indicating that the Big Bang theory is incorrect. Of course, this has vast implications, as it is from the basis of the Big Bang that current scientific teaching began. So, if critics in the scientific community deem the theories of Ronald Pearson (see Chapter 10) to be unacceptable, then by the same but opposite token, so must be the Big Bang theory to those of us who subscribe to alternative ideas such as those of Ronald Pearson. Indeed, the latest developments in the areas of quantum physics argue strongly for a connection and explanation linking both 'sides' of the otherwise seemingly irreconcilable arguments (see also **Paranormal Phenomenon**).

Cabinet – During the manifestations at a séance or sitting, the physical medium usually sits within an enclosed area, called a cabinet. This helps focus the energies and creates a type of battery, from which the phenomena can be built and energised. A curtain is usually placed across the front and this can be drawn back for people to see what is going on within the cabinet.

Chakra – Chakra is the Sanskrit word for 'moving wheel'. The chakras are vortices of energy present in the ethereal body and in related locations of the physical body. They bring in the universal energies we need to remain living. There are seven major chakras and they function as pathways for energy to be taken in, metabolised and sent to the major nerve centre nearest each one. Several more chakras seem to be opening up in many people but for now we will deal with the traditional seven.

The chakras are located along the line of the spinal

column and are composed of high-frequency energy strands that the spiritual eye perceives as light. The life force is channelled to the physical body and its organs via the meridians, and enters the body through the chakras. The degree of chakra activity depends on a combination of the physical, emotional, mental and spiritual development of the individual.

Disruption of the chakra and aura creates disease and disturbs the energy balance of the chakras. Chakras can be damaged or blocked through an emotional upset such as conflict, loss or accident. Fear, anxiety and stress are also common causes of chakra malfunction. Psychological problems may cause 'blockages', obstructing the flow of energy into or out of the chakras.

Circle / Home Circle – A circle of people sitting together trying to contact etheric people living in the next world. This practice is closely associated with Spiritualism, though not necessarily so. Usually, the séance will be held in a darkened room illuminated only by candles or red light – or, in the case where pure physical mediumship is being practised, pitch-blackness. Most mediums use specially adapted rooms or purpose-built quarters without windows or any form of natural light. The door is often sealed with strong adhesive tape, which also eliminates any potential of fraud, such as people entering purporting to be materialisations. There are various kinds of physical séances, some feature materialisation, others feature apports, and there are others that have the etheric people playing musical instruments. In the immediate post-war periods of the last century, séances were extremely popular as recently bereaved widows attempted to contact their deceased husbands. There are various reasons for the demise of this practise – lack of time, increase in working hours and man's obsession with the material world are some.

Circle A, B, C, D, etc. – My own terminology for the various physical circles operating in England at the time of writing this book.

Clairaudience / Clairsentience Clairaudience is when the medium hears the etheric person, and clairsentience is when the medium senses the presence and the thoughts of the etheric person. Mental phenomena of this type are those most often demonstrated in public. Mental mediumship takes place within the consciousness of the medium and the results are expressed verbally, passing through the medium's mouth.

Darkened Rooms / Light – In physical mediumship, is that of darkness most phenomena occur in darkened quarters with only an occasional dim red light or fluorescent paint on objects providing any light source. Natural or white light is said to inhibit the phenomena, while dim red light energises them. These conditions prevent people from seeing very well and can create a psychological effect, which provides the seeds for accusations that it is all a figment of the imagination. Different mediums and circles utilise different things in their sittings. Typical items could include a bell, a white sheet of paper with a pencil (for spirit writing) and trigger objects (where things are moved from fixed positions), drumsticks with luminous paint on the ends, rattles and musical instruments such as flutes and trumpets (again all dipped in luminous paint so when they move their motion can be witnessed).

Direct Voice and Independent Direct Voice – An incredible phenomenon. An ectoplasmic voice box is created by the etheric world, through which its inhabitants can speak physically and audibly to all who are present. By one circle, it is said to be a like an inverted pyramid in shape and is usually evident above the heads of the sitters. During direct voice the strength of the voice shifts as the energy levels and harmonies change. When it first begins, it is often very garbled and difficult to distinguish. As the energy is built up, it becomes more powerful and more easily understood. Towards the end of the session, when the energies begin to diminish, so too do the quality and clarity of the voice. In fact, this gradual peaking and diminishing of phenomena is quite common in all forms of physical manifestations. Sometimes, towards the end of a strong communication, the speech can become extremely rapid with no opportunity for the speaker to even take a breath, as they would have to do in this life.

A small conical device, known as a trumpet, is often used as an indicator or focus for the sitting group but is rarely an actual instrument of origin. If the energy is low the voice of an entity may be directed through the trumpet, which then acts very much like the cabinet, in that the energies are focussed inside it. The trumpet is often levitated around the room, with the etheric people speaking through it.

Ectoplasm – When the energy-matter is drawn from the

medium's body, it is known as ectoplasm. Ectoplasm is and can be drawn from the medium, sitters and indeed the materials in the room – for example, carpets, curtains, clothes and furniture. Only a small amount is taken, otherwise the source would disintegrate. In cases where there is a spontaneous ADC, with no medium present, the dead person appears as a vision. In these cases, the ectoplasm is drawn directly from the room (as recounted in my book *After Death Communication*). One circle with whom I am in touch reported that clothes worn during sittings wear out very quickly because of the ectoplasm.

It is through the use and manipulation of ectoplasm that the physical phenomena occur. Ectoplasm can be created in many different forms – visible and invisible, white and coloured – depending upon what the etheric people wish to do with it. Once created, it generally emerges from the medium through some bodily orifice (usually the nose or mouth) or through a 'psychic' centre, located near the navel, known as the solar plexus.

Ectoplasm can also be used to move objects. During a demonstration such as this, the etheric operator might mould the ectoplasm into hardened rods (see **Ectoplasmic Rods**) and direct these rods to the underside of an object and cause the object to be lifted. This is known as levitation and usually – although not always – involves the production of an invisible form of ectoplasm. Objects known to be levitated have ranged in weight from a few grams to hundreds of kilograms.

Ectoplasmic Rods – This is rare. However, some circles believe that the etheric people use the ectoplasm to create 'rods'. These are then used in physical circles to distribute energy among the participants and construct spiritual devices – like a voice box, which is then used to talk directly to circle members. I have been told that most people in the circle can see the rods from time to time, and sometimes they are more obvious than at others. The rods can be of different sizes, ranging from fine hair-like parallel lines, a cross-wire mesh, single rods of an eighth of an inch all the way through to examples an inch thick.

When people have these rods set in their body, they often experience discomfort. The common areas are the arms, legs, stomach and the back. The wrists are often used as an energy-gathering point. If somebody in the circle moves across these rods and breaks them, the sitter who has the rods attached usually experiences some discomfort as they are wrenched from his or her body – though some say the description of this sensation is exaggerated to ensure sitters do not fidget! However, of the developing and developed groups I have conversed with, only one discussed this form of usage. From what I have gathered, it may have been what was done in the early experiments, but the etheric scientists have improved their techniques out of all recognition. As with other circles, they now lift things, like we do, with their hands, so no discomfort is felt at all by the circle or guest sitters.

Ether – A substance that permeates space. This was done away with when Einstein's theory of relativity became accepted scientific teaching. Some consider this to be a terrible mistake, which has set scientific advancement back a hundred years. Without the ether – somewhere to go – there can be no question of survival after death. Scientific teaching across every discipline has eliminated the so-called spirit world. Ronald Pearson has brought back the ether, which he has renamed the 'i-ther' – intelligent ether. This fits in with experiments that prove the invisible part of the universe is teeming with 'life'. It is the source of all energy for our physical world.

Etheric Body – There are so many ways to describe this entity that vocabulary becomes a problem. It can also be referred to as the Spirit, Mind, Soul, Intelligence, Entity, Astral Body, Discarnate Entity, Consciousness or the Personality. However, all of these terms mean exactly the same thing – I have chosen to use the word *etheric*, to avoid religious connotations.

In essence, the etheric body is the part of us that lives on when we die. It is perfect in form. Therefore, for instance, if we lose a limb, then the etheric body retains it. This explains phantom limbs and visions of deceased loved ones appearing in full health, *not* with the pains of anguish or dismemberment that were there when they died. At the point of death, the etheric body separates from the old physical one. This is what can be seen as part of the aura – the etheric body.

Etheric World – The vibration, frequency or 'realm' that we pass into naturally upon death. It has been argued that the etheric world contains the oneness of consciousness that explains ESP, synchronicity and other 'psychic' phenomena that have amazed people for centuries. By understanding this it can be appreciated that the body acts simply as a gateway, as a communication tool, with the brain as a tuning device for focus and management of data between the etheric (spiritual) world and the physical one.

Experiment (Séance or Sitting) – The word séance comes from the Latin verb *sedere*, which means sitting. I refer here to the mediums who sit regularly with others in what is termed a séance or sitting. However, I have chosen to use the term 'experiment', rather than 'séance' or 'sitting', both of which have various unhelpful connotations – one does not need to be a Spiritualist nor have any religious belief to witness physical or materialisation phenomena. After all an experiment is, essentially, what it is; an experiment to link the two wavelengths – the one in which we reside and the etheric realms we pass into at death.

Of course, sittings differ from medium to medium and dependent on where they are being held and who is sitting. Even before a sitting, there are precautions, rules and terms to abide by, whether you are a guest sitter or circle member – this is as much for the safety of the medium as the sitter. Well-developed groups are more lenient in their rules, but a circle that is developing at the moment includes several guidelines such as only eating a light meal beforehand, wearing comfortable clothing (for the sitter's own comfort – some sittings can last several hours, which is a long time to be sat in the same seat in the dark), and being asked not to wear any jewellery or watches.

Force – What religionists call God, otherwise known by others as the Universe, the Power, and so on.

Ghosts (and **Apparitions**) – Ghosts are generally insubstantial and wraith-like and rarely communicate with the person or people who see them. In fact, they are usually quite unaware – or seem to be unaware – of the presence of those who observe them and are more preoccupied with their own thoughts and concerns. Therefore, the difference between ghosts and materialised etheric people is the fact that the materialised form, appearing through the agency of a strong medium or spontaneously as an ADC, is frequently (but not always) an integrated personality. It has intelligence and the ability to communicate and verbalise its thoughts. In addition, materialised forms, by their very nature, are much more solid in composition than ghosts and apparitions.

Guest Sitters (**Independent Witnesses**) – People who do not sit regularly as part of the group. Most often these are first-time sitters with no knowledge of the group or associated phenomena. Such people usually go along once or twice in the hope of meeting with or hearing from deceased loved ones or they go seeking personal proof of the afterlife. Physical mediumship is objective in nature; that is, when the phenomenon occurs, everyone in the room is able to see and/or hear it, unlike spontaneous apparitions, such as ghosts or ADC, which often appear to only one person. However, sceptics claim that the materialisation of etheric people is just trickery. Nevertheless, circles and sitters I have talked to say they make every effort to prove otherwise – the medium might be bound and gagged, their arms strapped with special one-way binds. I have been told that it is possible for a medium's cardigan to be turned inside out and back to front during a séance, even when they are fully bound, showing the effects of de- and re-materialising it.

The circle is arrranged with circle members and sitters interspersed and holding hands so all newcomers know that everyone is still. The door is taped so that no one can enter or leave. Then sitters are invited to view the cabinet and search the room. People who have witnessed the materialisation of deceased loved ones say that if there is a trick it is an extremely clever one and quite pointless. Most physical mediums charge very little, if anything, for their services and do it as a service to mankind to prove the truth of eternal life.

In a demonstration of mental mediumship, it is the medium who hears, sees and feels what the etheric communicators are relating. The sitters, or anyone else present, are unable to witness the phenomena. Furthermore, it is the medium's function to relate the information, with minimum personal influence and prejudice, to the recipient of the message, also known as the sitter. In a typical sitting, guest sitters are given a copy of the terms and conditions of the séance to agree and sign; sitters are then searched (physically and with a metal detector) to ensure that they do not have any torches, matches or video recording equipment (again because the potential luminosity is dangerous to the medium). One circle removes electronic watches, because the batteries have a tendency to drain; the group attributes this to sitters sometimes having bands of energy formed around their wrists, which can cause discomfort.

Independent direct voice – see Direct voice

Lucid Dreams – see **Astral Travel**

Materialisation and Etheric People – In materialisation, the etheric people use ectoplasm to create an image or moulding of themselves. The degree and strength of the materialised form varies quite a bit. A full-form, head-to-toe materialisation of an etheric person (otherwise called a spirit, known or unknown) is, perhaps, the most amazing phenomenon witnessed. This can happen spontaneously or in a particular situation. For example, in an ADC, a deceased person who is unknown to the recipient, might be seen at the foot of the bed saying goodbye. Later, the recipient finds out that the person they saw had died moments before they were visited.

Materialisations can also be induced during a séance or sitting via a medium. There are countless recorded cases where etheric people have materialised fully, with full dress and facial features. Some have been as clear and solid as an earthly body; some cases have even reported the fact that fingerprints had been created. Materialised etheric people have been known to walk among sitters; talk to them via direct voice; touch, hug, and kiss them; allow the sitters to touch and hold them; pass through walls and furniture, and dematerialise before the sitters.

A most interesting phenomenon seen during materialisation is the physical link between the materialised form and the medium. After an etheric person materialises and walks away from the medium, a cord of ectoplasm can be seen (and felt) linking the etheric form to the medium. This ectoplasmic cord can be likened to the umbilical cord of a foetus. Through it, the etheric operator receives a supply of etheric energy-matter from the medium. The etheric person may dematerialise by withdrawing the ectoplasm back into the medium's body via this cord. A specific form of materialisation, whereby the etheric operator uses the ectoplasm to mould his or her face over the face of the medium, is known as **transfiguration**.

Medium – Most words connected with mediumship tend to be very ambiguous and easily misconstrued. Words such as 'clairvoyants' and 'psychics' come complete with connotations of Hollywood-style images and crystal balls. It is for this reason, and also to stay away from Spiritualist jargon, that I have chosen to use the term 'medium'. When discussing the 'medium', I find it helpful to visualise them rather like a television set: they are the medium through which the invisible signals from the sender, or broadcaster, are viewed. In this case, however, the medium is the means by which those in the next world communicate.

There are many various forms of mediumship but all contain the basic element of communication between the medium and those alive in the world beyond. Some mediums have the gift of clairaudience, clairvoyance or clairsentience and they then pass these on to those sitting with them. Often, mediums work on a one-to-one basis, face-to-face, but some can work by remote means, such as over the telephone or more recently via an internet link with someone seeking their services. However, please be *very* careful of frauds pretending to be mediums who might be taking money from grieving people. Like plumbers and builders, it's always best to be guided by recommendations from others who have successfully made contact with their 'dead' loved ones.

Mediumship – This can best be categorised by two basic types, mental mediumship and physical mediumship, depending upon which type of phenomenon is being manifested. (See also **Mental Mediumship** and **Physical Mediumship**.)

Mental Mediumship – This involves the relating of information, through communication from the afterlife, via the varied aspects of thought transference, or mental telepathy. Mental telepathy is the relaying of information via thought, without using any of the five physical senses, and is purely demonstrated through the mind of the medium. It can be by clairvoyance that the medium sees the etheric person. (See also **Clairaudience / Clairsentience**.)

Mind – Otherwise called the soul, spirit, personality, ego, character, unconscious or conscious. However, *my* definition is based on the notion that the mind and brain are two differing and separate entities, with the mind being the part of us that drives the brain. In computer terminology, it could be said that the mind is the software and the brain is the hardware.

Near Death Experience (NDE) – A term coined by Raymond Moody to describe a series of life-changing visions experienced by a person (usually) on the point of death. The near-death phenomenon first came to light in 1977, when *Readers Digest* published, in condensed form, the book *Life After Life* by psychiatrist Dr Raymond Moody. What this new-found knowledge and interest in NDEs has created is the revival of interest in the age-old question about death and the possibility of an afterlife.

Out-of-Body Experience (OBE) – This experience occurs when a person's duplicate invisible body, sometimes called the astral body or etheric body, is able to move out of the physical body with full consciousness. For most people, there is no control at all over the OBE; it just happens. A person who experiences an OBE does *not* have to be ill or near death. Those who have had an OBE usually accept afterwards that they have survived physical death. They know that the reason why they return to their physical body is because their invisible duplicate body is still connected to the physical body by a silver cord. (This is a theory that is hearsay, passed on from the etheric word, but it makes sense to many people.) When the silver cord is irretrievably severed, the invisible (to physical eye) body continues to survive in the afterworld.

OBEs have been reported from all around the world for some 20 centuries, starting with accounts by Plato, Socrates and Pliny.

Paranormal – I am using the term given to things that seemingly cannot be explained by normal, objective methods. However, this book argues that there is no such thing as the paranormal.

Paranormal Phenomena / Psychic Phenomena – Professors Brian Josephson and Peter Wadhams, both from Cambridge University, have linked paranormal and psychic phenomena with the scientific discipline of quantum physics – the study of the subatomic part of the universe. These two brilliant professors are discovering some of the scientific principles underlying Sir William Crookes' experiments in materialisation undertaken last century. Because of the answers found in this branch of physics, we can now begin to account logically for so-called 'paranormal' activity: that is we no longer need to describe anything as 'paranormal' or 'supernatural', as it is now being demonstrated to be natural and normal. Excitingly, it is from this development that we can begin to explain the existence of an afterlife, visions of deceased loved ones, psychokinesis, ESP and so forth.

Physical Circle – Physical circles are very different to what would normally be termed a clairvoyant or healing circle. Physical circles are very draining on the individuals involved and it is imperative that the correct 'mix' of people is obtained energywise. Sometimes, finding this mix can take years. An abundance of ectoplasm energy is required to allow material manifestation. Different circles use the energy in many different ways. In some, the energy is used to construct rods on the etheric side, which are then inserted into the participating sitter's bodies to collect the energy required for the circle (see **Ectoplasmic Rods**). I find this rod element to be a rare one, most circle's energy is obtained from the playing of loud music and singing to heighten the vibrations and create energy, and during the sitting no discomfort is felt by anyone present.

Physical Medium – Not everyone can become a physical medium. Unlike evidential mediumship (mediumship which provides evidence of an afterlife), which can, to some degree, be developed within most people, physical mediumship requires certain elements to be present within the physical organism of the medium. Either you have those elements or you do not. In a nutshell, a physical medium is someone who is able to produce **ectoplasm**, a physical substance that is created by the energy from the body, which allows etheric entities either to create a voice-box type device through which they can talk or to materialise a full body (rarely) or sometimes (more often) bodily parts, like a hand, or a face that people can see or touch.

Physical mediums must have an abundance of what is known as etheric matter within the ether regions or 'etheric body'. (This is explained more fully later, when we explore the differing layers of the aura. The ether is the first layer surrounding our physical bodies and is a subtle counterpart of the physical body. From this, it is clear that mediumship involves a cooperative effort between a person on earth (the medium, or channel) and a person in the etheric world (the communicator or operator).

There are several objectives behind the manifestation of mediumship. In addition to this, we see that mediumship is used by those in the etheric world for the following purposes:

- To cause certain types of 'paranormal' activities to occur.
- To channel forth certain types of energies.
- To manifest themselves materially.
- To present information, which may or may not be verifiable.

Apparently, there is no limit to what the etheric people can do, provided the proper conditions prevail. In the case of physical sittings (see **Experiments**), I had heard from witnesses who have described an array of happenings, the main one being the manipulation of ectoplasm: this is the most fundamental use of ectoplasm. The ectoplasm is released from the medium's body, and the operator demonstrates how it can be fashioned and directed. This becomes a demonstration of etheric person's ability to influence matter via the directed use of mind.

Physical Mediumship – Because of its nature, physical mediumship is usually only demonstrated at private séances. Any person sitting with the medium can hear or see what is happening – this can be by means of raps, audible voices or materialised figures. It is a form of mediumship that can produce physical phenomena including full and partial materialisation. This is the formation of a seemingly solid, or semi-solid, figure of a dead person (or indeed animal).

Physical mediumship usually involves ectoplasm. One theory is that ectoplasm allows intelligences from the afterlife to reduce their vibrations to the physical human level. When there is sufficient ectoplasm, an etheric person can materialise and become solid. Pets and loved ones who have died become recognizable. Just as people have seen ghosts throughout the millennia and have reported ADC with deceased loved ones, these etheric people, some known, some not known, but all traceable individuals, come back to our reality in this experimental setting. The etheric people convey intimate information about themselves, their recollection of their earthly lives and details of their lives in the etheric world. Often the materialised shape can be touched and may feel real. Wax impressions have even been taken of their hands, which show real fingerprints. There may be a distinct pungent smell in the vicinity of a materialisation. Sounds and often voices may emit from the materialised form.

I have heard and been sent testimonies of deep philosophical conversations that have taken place between sitters and the etheric people. This is the reason why this type of mediumship is so attractive to the scientific community. In physical mediumship, the medium is a totally passive instrument and takes no part in the conversations between the etheric people and their contacts on earth. The etheric operators use this person's abundance of etheric energy and matter to produce the various manifestations. They do this exactly as Anton Mesmer (the discoverer of hypnotism) observed: releasing it through the directed use of mind (see Chapter 6). The implications are quite staggering: mind is capable of affecting matter. Perhaps this is the most pertinent implication lying at the foundation of physical mediumship.

Sitters have told me that the medium's mind had no input whatsoever during this process – they were talking directly with the etheric people and not via the medium. Most often, although not always, the medium must be in a state of deep trance. This helps place their mind on the sideline, so to speak, thus allowing the intelligence of the etheric operator to work with and manipulate the etheric energy-matter. The etheric people have explained that they assist the medium in attaining this trance state through a process not unlike that of Mesmer's magnetic passes (see Chapter 6).

Physical or Material Body – Quite simply the shell we live in – our spacesuits for our time on earth. It is believed that this physical body is connected to the etheric body by a chord. The etheric people tell us that, at the moment of death, the cord breaks and the etheric body – along with the mind, which is a part of it – withdraws from the physical form and moves onto another wavelength (or dimension), there to continue its evolution.

Psi – Anomalous processes of information or energy transfer (such as telepathy or other forms of extrasensory perception) that are currently unexplained in terms of known physical or biological mechanisms.

Raps and Taps – This is a common form of activity observed in circles for physical mediumship. The etheric people cause sharp raps to be heard, often from within the table the circle is sitting around. A code can be established through the raps, thus creating a means of conveying specific messages to the sitters.

Séance – see **Experiment**

Sitting – see **Experiment**

Solar Plexus – A network of nerves behind the stomach and an important chakra. It's the centre of our being. When you feel sick or nervous, in love or anxious, this is why you feel it in the stomach. It is a sensitive area, being the root of fight or flight. It is also a very receptive area in mediumship as it is often a point where ectoplasm is generated, although this does vary from person to person.

Spirit Lights or **Etheric Lights / Orbs** – This is another common occurrence in physical circles. Flashes or balls of light (energy) appear, often on or near the vicinity of the medium.

Transfiguration – In one circle, the ectoplasm is used to construct the faces of the etheric people who have come through, using a sitter's face as a template. It is very interesting to see this in the circle, as everyone sees the same thing. Usually, a person is selected as a transfiguration sitter, either by another sitter or by the medium. The etheric people then use the collected ectoplasm to construct a physical facemask in front of the chosen sitter. An etheric person will move in from behind the transfiguration sitter and push their face into the mask, thus moulding his or her image in front of the sitter. As this happens, hair can change, people may grow beards or moustaches, while their face becomes fatter or thinner, and the sitter can have more than one face coming over their own quite rapidly. The faces are very distinct when they form. The sitters who are looking on normally agree about the features of each face they see, proving that it is not a trick of the light or somebody's imagination.

Xenoglossy – The ability to speak fluently in a foreign language or strange tongue – sometimes modern and other times a *dead language* – while in an altered state of consciousness. The important point is that the person speaking has no knowledge whatsoever of that language when fully conscious.

NOTES AND REFERENCES

Preface
(1) It is for this reason that I am careful with my choice of words. Emotive words such as 'séance' conjure up ridiculous images for most people and I have chosen to use scientific words instead as this is my approach to the phenomenon. I shall refer to work with a medium as an experiment and at times use the word 'ether' or 'etheric' to describe what is commonly labelled soul/spirit/guide/ghost/energy as per the glossary.

Chapter 1
(1) Adapted from
http://liftoff.msfc.nasa.gov/academy/universe/b_bang.html
(2) Boddington, Harry, *Materializations*, Psychic Press, London 1992; p.10

Chapter 2

(1) This section was taken, with permission, from
Zammit, Victor, *A Lawyer's Case for the Afterlife*, which relied
on the Zeitschrift für Parapsychologie publication O
Medium Mirabelli, 1927; pp. 450–462. A copy of this book is
held in the British Library in London.

(2) Inglis, Brian, *Science and Parascience – A History of the
Paranormal 1914–1939*, Hodder & Stoughton London,
1984; p. 223.

(3) Inglis, Brian *Science and Parascience – A History of the
Paranormal 1914–1939*, Hodder & Stoughton, London,
1984; p. 226.

(4) Edwards, Harry, *The Mediumship of Jack Webber*, Rider,
London, 1940. Much can be pulled off the internet from a
simple name search. Also see The Noah's Ark Society
website for biographies of past materialisation and
physical mediums: http://www.noahsarksoc.co.uk

(5), (6), (7) & (8) Harris, Louie, *They Walked Among Us*,
Psychic Press Ltd, London, 1980.

Chapter 3

(1) Marris, P, *Widows and Their Families* RKP, London,
1958.

(2) Parkes, CM, 'Bereavement and Mental Illness' in *British
Journal of Medical Psychology*, 38, (1) 1965.

(3) Adapted from:
http://paranormal.about.com/library/weekly/aa021901a.htm

(4) Davies, Duglas, *Death, Ritual and Belief*, Cassell,
London, 1997.

(5) Cleiren, M, *Adaptation after Bereavement*, Leiden
University Press, Leiden 1991; p.129.

(6) Moody, Raymond, *Reunions*, Warner, 1996. Widows were selected for these studies simply because women tend to outlive men, so there are more widows making them more accessible for study.

(7) Finucane, RC, *Appearances of the Dead: A Cultural History of Ghosts*, Junction Books, London, 1982; p. 223.

(8) Adapted from: Hooper, John, 'Dialogue with the Dead is Feasible', London *Observer* Service.

(9) Department of Sociology & Anthropology, Trinity University, Texas.

Chapter 4
(1) Read the full evidence on the website:
www.victorzammit.com

(2) Used with permission from Victor Zammit, see also his website above.

(3) See Tom Wright's book *For All the Saints*, SPCK, London, 2003.

Chapter 5
(1) Adapted with permission from Leroy Kattein:
www.ndeweb.com/wildcard

Chapter 6
(1) See website where it will be transcripted:
www.cfpf.org.uk

(2) & (3) Greber, Johannes, *Communication with the Spirit World of God – Personal Experiences of a Catholic Priest*, Memorial Foundation, 139 Hillside Avenue, Teaneck, New Jersey 07666, USA, 1970; p. 236.

(4) See website:
http://www.childpastlives.org/stevenson.htm
(5) Idea taken from Trinkett, Shirley, *Coping with Anxiety and Depression*, a part of the 'Overcoming Common Problems' series, Sheldon Press, London, 1996; page 71.
(6) As above; page 48.
(7) Sheldrake, Rupert in 'Phantom Limbs: Do Minds Reach Out from our Brains'; part of his seven experiment series of papers to be found on the website:
www.sheldrake.org/experiments/phantom
(8) 'The Folklore of Phantoms'; a section of the Rupert Sheldrake paper as above.
(9) Carrington, Hereward, *The World of Psychic Research*, AS Barns & Co Inc, New Jersey, 1973.
(10) As available on the website: http://www.near-death.com/experiences/experts09.html
(11) Sheldrake, Rupert; as (7) above and also on website: www.transaction.net/science/seven/limb.html

Chapter 7

(1) Taken with permission from 'Alan Crossley Returns' *Psychic News*, 31 May, 2003.
(2) Edwards, H, *The Mediumship of Jack Webber*, The Healer Publishing Co, 1961.
(3) Notzing, Baron Von Schrenck, *Phenomena of Materialisations*, Routledege, London, 1923.

Chapter 8

(1) Adapted from: Roll, Michael, *A Rational Scientific Explanation For So-called Psychic Phenomena*; unpublished at time of going to print; revised January 2004.

(2) & (3) 'Materialised Figures Appear at Home Circle'
Psychic' News, No 2646
(4) Reproduced with the kind permission of Alan Cleaver.
A complete account of this meeting between 'dead' mother
and daughter is given in Issue 3 of *Anomaly*, journal of the
Association of the Scientific Study of Anomalous
Phenomena (ASSAP) in March 1987.
(5) Reproduced with permission from George Cranley,
report first printed in *The Paranormal Times*.
(6) This article by Ron Gilkes appeared in the *Ark Review*
of January/February 2000; reproduced with permission
from The NAS.

Chapter 10
(1) Taken from interviews and conversation with Ronald
Pearson and using adapted and abridged paragraphs from
Tom Bates 'The Science of Life after Death' in *Reflections*,
August, 2002.

Chapter 11
(1) Based on original paper by Rory McQuisten; since
revised during conversations and interviews with Ronald
Pearson, February 2004.
(2) Pearson, Ronald D, 'Alternative to Relativity including
Quantum Gravitation' presented at the Second
International Conference on Problems in Space and Time,
St Petersburg, Petrovskaja Academy of Sciences of Arts,
1991.
(3) Pearson, Ronald D,'Quantum Gravitation and the
Structured Ether' presented at the Sir Isaac Newton
Conference, St Petersburg, Petrovskaja Academy of

Sciences of Arts, March 1993. Chairman Local Organising
Committee: Dr Michael Varin Pulkovskoye Road, 65-9-1,
St Petersburg, 196140, Russia.

(4) Pearson, Ronald D, 'Problem of the Binary Pulsar'
presented at the Problems of Space, Time and Gravitation
Conference, 22–27 May, 1994 St Petersburg, Russia;
pp.103–108. Address as above.

(5) Pearson, Ronald D, 'Consciousness as a Sub-Quantum
Phenomenon' in *Frontier Perspectives*, Spring–Summer 1997,
Vol 6, N. 2, pp 70–78.

RESOURCES, ORGANISATIONS AND CONTACTS

Internet Sites

Please note that, while all sites were up and running at the
time of publication, it is not unusual for internet addresses
to change or go offline without warning.

Campaign for Philosophical Freedom www.cfpf.org.uk
The Campaign for Philosophical Freedom is a non-profit
organisation founded by Michael Roll to present the
secular scientific case for survival after death.

Noah's Art (Ark) Society www.noahsarksoc.co.uk
A worldwide Educational Society for the Promotion,
Development and Safe Practice of Physical Mediumship.
This site has extensive articles on past materialisation
mediums and the afterlife.

After-Death Communication: www.after-death.com
Huge resource site for both grief and belief by Bill & Judy
Guggenheim, authors of *Hello From Heaven* and of the
foreword for my last book *After Death Communication*.

Near Death Experience: www.near-death.com
Possibly the most comprehensive resource on near-death
experiences on the internet, and an excellent source for
'grief and belief' insight.

Dr Raymond Moody: www.lifeafterlife.com
Author of *Life After Life*, researcher and expert on near-
death experiences, Raymond A Moody, PhD, MD, has
25 years' experience of helping the bereaved. His books
are an excellent resource to establish *The Grief And Belief
Connection*.

Dr Brian Weiss: www.brianweiss.com
A graduate of Columbia University and Yale Medical
School, Brian L Weiss, MD, is an author of several top-
selling books based on his experience as a psychiatrist and
healer using past-life regression techniques including the
bestseller *Many Lives, Many Masters* – a must-read for anyone
seeking *The Grief And Belief Connection*.

Dr Elisabeth Kubler-Ross: www.elisabethkublerross.com
A psychiatrist and the author of the groundbreaking
On Death and Dying. Now in her 70s, she is a long-time
respected authority on the subject of death, dying and
grief.

Victor Zammit: www.victorzammit.com/book/index.html
Lawyer Victor Zammit presents 23 areas of evidence for
an afterlife in his free online book *A Lawyer Presents The Case
For The Afterlife.*

The Kevin Nunan Foundation: www.survivalscience.org
Scientific support for evidence-based mediumship, life
after death and after-death communication. Great website
for people needed scientific evidence to establish *The Grief
And Belief Connection.*

Dr Melvin Morse: www.melvinmorse.com/light.htm
A paediatrician and neuroscientist who spent 15 years
studying the NDE of children. He has learned that the
final moments of life are not frightening. Comforting
resource for the grieving.

Institute for Afterlife Research:
www.mikepettigrew.com/afterlife
Presents evidence for the survival of physical death based
on the experiences of thousands of people from around
the world.

Dr Ian Stevenson /www.childpastlives.org/stevenson.htm
Trying to get the word out about the scientific evidence
for reincarnation. This website devotes a whole section to
articles by and about Stevenson, and gives guidance and
links to anyone interested in going to the source and
reading his books. The Reincarnation Forum has a special
Dr Ian Stevenson Forum for sharing thoughts on what this
all means.

Betty Eadie: www.embracedbythelight.com
This author's book, *Embraced By The Light*, sold more than 6 million copies, stayed on the *New York Times* bestseller list for more than two years, and brought comfort and hope to millions of people by sharing the story of her near-death experience. Highly recommended book for *The Grief And Belief Connection*.

PMH Atwater: www.cinemind.com/atwater
One of the original researchers in the field of near-death studies who began her work in 1978. Five books have been published since then about her amazing findings. Any of her books can be helpful for grief healing.

BeliefNet.com: www.beliefnet.com
A great site for both grief and belief articles. This link goes to the *Angels and Guides* section, but check out their *Grief and Loss* section too.

Crossing Over With John Edward:
www.scifi.com/johnedward/aboutjohn
Possibly the best television show on TV to help you learn about life after death and overcome scepticism.

The Interview With God: www.interviewwithgod.com
A website that hosts a beautiful and powerfully moving presentation 'to help us feel a little closer to heaven... a gentle reminder that we are not alone.' Excellent for grief healing. Be sure to click on the *Presentation*.

1000deaths: www.1000deaths.com
The 'Survivors Of Loved One's Suicides' fellowship
(SOLOS) offers this website for people dealing with the
loss of a loved one due to suicide. 1000deaths.com and
SOLOS.org are combined (connected) depending on
which link you choose.

BabySteps: www.babysteps.com
Named after the baby steps that form the long and
difficult road to recovery from the loss of a child and aims
to care for the support and informational needs of
bereaved parents and their communities.

WidowNet: www.fortnet.org/widownet
An information and self-help resource for, and by, widows
and widowers. Topics covered include grief, bereavement,
recovery, and other information helpful to people of all
ages, religious backgrounds and sexual orientations, who
have suffered the death of a spouse or life partner.

Merry Widow: www.merrywidow.me.uk
Written by Kate Boydell who was widowed at the age of
33. Kate is the author of *Big Hearted Man* and on her
website has written a practical guide for women in her
position who need clear, simple, advice.

Petloss: www.petloss.com
A gentle and compassionate website for pet lovers who are
grieving over the death of a pet or an ill pet.

Association for Pet Loss and Bereavement: www.aplb.org
The APLB is a compassionate non-profit organization
dedicated to helping people with bereavement in response
to pet loss.

The Compassionate Friends:
www.compassionatefriends.org
A national non-profit, self-help support organisation that
offers friendship and understanding to bereaved parents,
grandparents and siblings. There is no religious affiliation
and there are no membership dues or fees.

GriefNet: www.griefnet.org
An Internet community for people dealing with grief,
death, and major loss. They have 47 e-mail support groups
and two websites (one for children). Their integrated
approach to online grief support provides help to people
working through various loss and grief issues.

AARP Grief and Loss Programs:
www.aarp.org/griefandloss/about.html
Offers a wide variety of resources and information on
bereavement issues for adults of all ages and their families.
Services include: one-to-one peer outreach, a grief course,
bereavement support groups, informational booklets and
brochures, and online support.

Rainbows: www.rainbows.org
A site for adults wanting to learn how to best help
children recover after experiencing loss. A child's grieving
process is different to that of adults. Helpful resource for
helping children who suffer from any loss-related issues.

Emma Heathcote-James

In-sight Books: www.insightbooks.com
Publisher founded by Doug Manning, offers books, videos
and cassettes in the areas of bereavement, elder care,
nursing homes and funeral services that have touched over
a million people since 1983.

Organisations and Societies

Arthur Findlay College & The Spiritualist National Union
Redwoods, Stanstead Hall,
Stanstead, Essex CM24 8UD
Tel: 01279 816 363
snu@snu.org.uk www.snu.org.uk
College of Psychic Studies
16, Queensbury Place,
London SW7 2EB
Tel: 0207 589 3292

Churches Fellowship for Psychical/Spiritual Studies
(CFPSS)
The Rural Workshop
South Road
North Somercotes
Nr Louth
Lincolnshire LN11 7PT
Tel: 0507 358 845
gensec@cfpss.freeserve.co.uk
The Christian Parapsychologist and *The Quarterly Review*

International Association for Near Death Studies
Lesser Hailings
Tile House Lane
Nr Uxbrige
Middlesex. UB9 5 DG
Tel: 01895 835 818

Society for Psychical Research (SPR)
49, Marloes Road,
London W8 6LA
Tel: 0207 937 8984
uksociety@aol.com
Produces the *Journal for Society for Psychical Research*
and *The Paranormal Review*

BIBLIOGRAPHY

As WITH ADC, relatively little has been written on the topic of physical mediumship. However, I have included a variety of books and articles here, some of which take a lay approach to the questions of life after death while others take a more scientific or philosophical approach. They are not meant to be on a par with each other, nor am I necessarily in agreement with every author though I do believe that they will provide the inquisitive reader with many rich hours of study.

I would recommend getting your hands on a copy of Robin Foye's *Physical Mediumship* and a copy of the SPR's *Scole Report. The Mediumship of Jack Webber* by Harry Edwards is an interesting place to begin and glean much insight. Arthur Findlay's *On the Edge of the Etheric* may be obtained through the Arthur Findlay College. 01279 813 636.

There's also Anthony Borgia's *Life in the World Unseen* and anything by Silver Birch (for example *Lift Up Your Hearts, The Seed of Truth, Silver Birch Companion, Silver Birch Speaks* and others).

Almeder, Robert, *Beyond Death*, Charles C Thomas, 1987.

Bache, Christopher, *Lifecycles: Reincarnation and the Web of Life*, Paragon House, 1991

Baird, John Logie. 'Sermons, Soap and Television'. In a paper presented from the estate of Logie Baird's library to the Royal Television Society, 1988. The inventor of television tells how fingerprints taken at a materialisation experiment matched the prints on the dead physical body.

Barbanell, Maurice, *The Case of Helen Duncan*, Psychic Book Club, London, 1945.

Borysenko, Joan, *Minding the Body, Mending the Mind*, Addison- Wesley, 1987.

Byrne, Gwen, *Russell*, Janus, 1994. (Gwen has now republishedthis herself. Price including post and packing £7.99 with cheques payable to Gwen Byrne at 62 Station Crescent, Rayleigh, Essex SS6 8AR, UK This mother tells how she and her family have been physically reunited with her 'dead' son in scores of repeatable experiments.)

Comparetti, Domenico, *Virgil in the Middle Ages*, GE Stechert, New York, 1908.

Crookes, William, 'Experimental Investigation of a New Force' in *Quarterly Journal of Science*, July 1871.

Crookes, William, 'Specialist of Specialists?' in *Quarterly Journal of Science*, 1874. (Crookes defending himself after an anonymous attack was published in the *Quarterly Review* by a biologist from London University, Professor WB Carpenter. Also reproduced in full on the website www.cfpf.org.uk.)

Crossley, Alan E, *The Story of Helen Duncan*, Arthur H. Stockwell, 1975.

Ducasse, CJ, *A Critical Examination of the Belief in a Life After Death*, Charles C Thomas, no date.

Edwards, H, *The Mediumship of Jack Webber*, The Healer Publishing Co, 1961.

Essen, Louis, 'Relativity – Joke or Swindle?' in *Electronics & Wireless World*. (This criticism of Einstein's theory of relativity by the inventor of the atomic clock is censored in all mainstream scientific publications).

Feynman, Richard P, *QED*, Princeton University Press, Princeton, 1985.

Findlay, Arthur, *Rock of Truth*, Psychic Press, London, 1933.

Findlay, Arthur, *The Unfolding Universe*, Psychic Press, London, 1935.

Findlay, Arthur, *The Psychic Stream or The Source and Growth of the Christian Faith*, Psychic Press, London, 1939.

Findlay, Arthur, *The Curse of Ignorance: a History of Mankind*, (two vols), Psychic Press, London, 1947.

Findlay, Arthur, *On the Edge of the Etheric*, Psychic Press, London, 1931. Now available from the Psychic News Bookshop, Clock Cottage, Stanstead Hall, Stanstead, Essex CM24 8UD, UK at £9).

Fiore, Edith, PhD, *The Unquiet Dead*, Ballantine, New York, 1987.

Grof, Stan, *Beyond the Brain: Birth, Death and Transcendence in*

Psychotherapy, State University of New York Press, 1986 (Grof did some of the well-documented pioneering research with LSD with thousands of subjects back in the 1960s, and later found that – essentially – the same results could be achieved without the use of drugs. This led to his development of a model of therapy designed to do just this kind of transformational work).

Hamilton, T Glen, *Intention and Survival*, Regency Press, 1942 (This describes the Canadian experiments).

Johnson, Paul, *A History of Christianity*, Weidenfeld & Nicolson, London, 1976.

Keen, M, Fontana, D & Ellison, A, 'The Scole Report', *Proceedings of the Society for Psychical Research*, Vol 58, pt 220, 1999

Koestler, Arthur, *The Roots of Coincidence*, Hutchinson, London, 1972.

Kubler-Ross, Elizabeth, *Death: The Final Stage of Growth*, Prentice-Hall, Inc, 1975.

Laurikainen, KV, 'Science Has Its Limits, Ontological Implications of Quantum Theory', University of Oulu Series in Physical Sciences, Report No 8, 1997.

Lenz, Frederick, *Lifetimes: True Accounts of Reincarnation*, Ballantine, New York, 1979 (like Fiore and Wambach, Lenz states he is not intending to prove or disprove reincarnation, but merely to present the accounts of experiences of other people).

Lodge, Oliver, 'The Mode of Future Existence', paper presented in 1933 at the Queen's Hospital Annual, Birmingham (this article by the inventor of radio links survival after death with subatomic physics. Lodge transmitted a radio message one year *before* Marconi).

Lodge, Oliver, *Ether and Reality*, Hodder & Stoughton, London, 1925.

Lodge, Sir Oliver, *Phantom Walls*, Hodder & Stoughton, London, 1929

Medhurst, RG, *Crookes and the Spirit World*, Souvenir Press, London, 1972.

Milton, Richard, *Forbidden Science*, Fourth Estate, London, 1994.

Montgomery, Ruth, and Garland, Joanne, *Ruth Montgomery: Herald of the New Age*, Ballantine, New York, 1986 (this volume provides an overview of her dozen other books).

Moody, Raymond A Jr, *Beyond the Light*, publisher unknown, 1988.

Moody, Raymond A Jr, *Coming Back: A Psychiatrist Explores Past-Life Journeys*, Bantam, New York, 1991 (Moody earned his doctorate from the University of Virginia, where Ian Stevenson also taught).

Moody, Raymond A, Jr, *Life After Life*, Mockingbird Press, 1975 (like Sabom's book on the topic, this is one of the classics that first laid out the characteristics of the near death experience. In his recent book, *The Last Laugh*, he cautions the reader that the two books need to be read together).

Moody, Raymond A, Jr, *Reflections on Life After Life*, Bantam, New York, 1977 (his sequel has some interesting things to say about suicide).

Myss, Caroline, *Anatomy of the Spirit: The Seven Stages of Power and Healing*, Bantam, New York, 1997 (includes a discussion of ways to understand the interconnections among the Hindu chakras, the Kabbalah's tree of life and the Christian sacraments).

Notzing, Baron Von Schrenck, *Phenomena of Materialisations*, Routledege, London, 1923 (translated by Paul Trench Trubner, this is an account of the German experiments).

Olson, Bob, *Medium Rare: A Skeptic's Journey Into The World Of Psychic Mediums And The Afterlife*; no other details avilable.

Ortzen, Tony (ed), *More Philosophy of Silver Birch*, Spiritualist Press, 1979.

Ostrander, Sheila, and Schroeder, Lynn, *Psychic Discoveries Behind the Iron Curtain*, Bantam, New York, 1971.

Paine, Thomas, *The Age of Reason*, 1793 (many versions available). Reprinted Citadel Press, New Jersey, 1949.

Pearson, Ronald D, 'An Alternative to Relativity Including Quantum Gravitation'. Published by The Russian Academy of Sciences, St. Petersburg, 1993, following presentation at the Second International Conference on Space and Time Problems in Modern Natural Science, 1992.

Pearson, Ronald D, 'Quantum Gravitation and the Structured Ether'. Published in 1994 By The Russian Academy of Sciences following the Sir Isaac Newton Conference held in 1993, St Petersburg.

Pearson, Ronald D, *Intelligence Behind The Universe*, Headquarters Publishing, 1990.

Pearson, Ronald D, *Origin of Mind*, a booklet based upon his paper 'Consciousness as a Sub-quantum Phenomenon', peer-refereed and published in the journal *Frontier Perspectives*, Temple University, Philadelphia, USA. Vol 6. No 2, spring–summer, 1997; pp 70–78.

Plowden Report, Vol 1, Central Advisory Council for Education, HMSO, UK, 1967.

Redfield, James, *The Celestine Prophecy*, Warner, 1993 (some love it, some hate it; it does a nice job of presenting a

range of 'paranormal' type possibilities – then there is the
sequel for those wanting more direction on how to
develop some of the skills described in the original
book).

Richet, Charles, *Thirty Years of Psychical Research*, Collins,
1923 (the Nobel Laureate for Medical Science describes
the French experiments).

Ring, Kenneth, *Heading Toward Omega: In Search of the Meaning
of the Near-Death Experience*, Morrow, New York, 1985
(compares near death experiences with the *kundalini*
phenomenon from Eastern mystics).

Riva, Pam (ed), *Light from Silver Birch*, Psychic Press, London,
1983.

Rogo, D Scott, *Leaving the Body, A Complete Guide to Astral
Projection*, Prentice-Hall, 1983.

Roll, Michael, 'A Rational Scientific Explanation for So
Called Psychic Phenomena' (available free of charge
via a stamped addressed envelope to Michael Roll at 12a
Westover Rise, Westbury on Trym, Bristol, BS9 3LU, UK).

Roll, Michael, 'The Scientific Proof of Survival After Death'
(a booklet sent free of charge as above).

Roll, Michael, 'Families Physically Reunited After Death', in
Psychic News, 12 September, 1992.

Roller, Gilbert, *A Voice From Beyond*, Popular Library, New
York, 1975.

Sabom, Michael B, 'Recollections of Death: A Medical
Investigation' in *Induced Dreams: About the Theory and
Therapeutic Applications of Dreams Hypnotically Induced*, Simon
& Sacerdote (eds), Theo Gaus, 1967 (instead of dealing
with dream recall in therapy sessions, Sacerdote helped
patients 'dream' during the session. Past-life therapy can

be understood as an extension of this concept, leaving open the question of whether to understand the 'dream' as the patient's projective metaphor, or as factual information from another lifetime).

Sagan, Carl, *Cosmos*, Abacus, London, 1983.

Stevenson, Ian, *Reincarnation and Biology: A Contribution to the Etiology of Birthmarks and Birth Defects*, Vols I and II, Praeger, 1997.

Stevenson, Ian, *Where Reincarnation and Biology Intersect*, Praeger, 1997.

Stevenson, Ian, 'American Children Who Claim to Remember Previous Lives', in *Journal of Nervous and Mental Disease*, 1983, 171; pp 742–748.

Stevenson, Ian, *Children Who Remember Previous Lives: A Question of Reincarnation*, University Press of Virginia, 1987 (Stevenson has devoted much of his career to researching this issue and this volume provides both the background and scientific research involved).

Stevenson, Ian, 'The Explanatory Value of the Idea of Reincarnation' in *Journal of Nervous and Mental Disease*, 164 (5), 1977; pp 305–326 (a good article summarising some of the issues).

Stevenson, Ian, 'Research into the Evidence of Man's Survival After Death' in *Journal of Nervous and Mental Disease*, 165 (3), 1977; pp 152–170.

Stevenson, Ian, *Unlearned Language: New Studies in Xenoglossy*, University Press of Virginia, 1977.

Stockwood, Mervyn, *Lord Bishop of Southwark* WH Allen, London, 1974.

Talbot, Michael, *Holographic Universe* (requires rather slow, careful reading. Presents a wealth of carefully referenced research in a fascinating model of how to understand the brain, the individual, and the illusion of separateness between physical reality and internal reality).

Tester, M H, *But What Do We Tell the Children*, Psychic Press, London, 1976.

Toland, John, *Adolf Hitler*, Doubleday, New York, 1976.

Twigg, Ena, *Medium An Autobiography*, WH Allen, London, 1973.

Von Schrenck-Notzing, B, *The Phenomena of Materialisation*, 1923, translated by Fournier d'Albe, Ayer, New York, 1975.

Walsch, Neal, *Conversations With God*, Hodder Mobius, London 1997 (I have found readers to have strongly divergent opinions about Walsch's books. For clinicians, these books offer another tool for understanding and integrating spirituality and clinical interventions. His later *Communion With God*, Hodder Mobius, London, 2000, deals with a set of ten illusions and the impact they have in how people perceive life).

Wambach, Helen, *Life Before Life*, Bantam, New York, 1979.

Warrick, FW, *Experiments in Psychics*, Rider, London, 1939.

Wilber, Ken, *The Spectrum of Consciousness*, Theosophical Publishing House/Quest Books, London, 1985.

Zammit, Victor, *A Lawyer Presents the Case for the Afterlife: Irrefutable Objective Evidence*, on website: http://www.victorzammit.com

Audio-visual

The Science of Eternity. Alan Pemberton's 1994 privately-produced and marketed video.

EMMA HEATHCOTE-JAMES

Other books

Seeing Angels

For the past three years, Emma Heathcote-James has been researching a phenomenon that has not, as yet, been studied seriously. Hundreds of British people have claimed to have experienced visions of angels. These people are not crazy new-age loonies, but ordinary people from all walks of life, from professionals to prisoners to children. Emma Heathcote-James is a 27-year-old theology graduate whose research for a PhD into contemporary experiences of angels is re-written here in layman's terms. Her findings are groundbreaking and unique and include more than 350 fascinating accounts which she has analysed in depth.

After Death Communication

This isn't about the usual psychics, mediums and séances which are so often talked about when discussing communications from beyond the grave. Rather, an After Death Communication (or ADC) is an experience which occurs when a person is contacted directly and spontaneously by a deceased family member or friend, without the use of psychics, mediums, rituals, or devices. ADCs are probably as old as mankind, yet Emma Heathcote-James has written the first UK-published book exploring the phenomenon, outlining accounts from hundreds of British people who have reported having these one-off spiritual encounters. ADCs offer dramatic new evidence of life after death with a staggering one in five people (or 20 per cent of the population) estimated to have had an ADC at some point in their life. These experiences are extremely common and, in many other parts of the world, are accepted as real communications. The accounts are deeply poignant and comforting. They offer powerful emotional and spiritual healing, especially for those who are grieving or afraid of death. Many reveal information the people did not know – and could not have known – before their ADCs occurred.

Psychic Pets

Psychic Pets looks at testimonies of animals who have performed exceptional acts of compassion, protection, healing, courage, or have been part of a miraculous or mystical experience.

BIOGRAPHY

BORN IN BIRMINGHAM in 1977, Emma's interests in the phenomenon of religion became apparent in her school days, leading to a degree in Theology at the University of Birmingham with research findings from her undergraduate studies in religious experience extended to a Masters degree and then the PhD from which her first bestselling book *Seeing Angels* arose. A BBC *Everyman* documentary was dedicated to her research and she has since written *After Death Communication* from which *They Walk Among Us* stemmed.

She has been a guest on Radio 4's *Womens Hour*, *Talksport*, *BBC World* and Radio 2's *Johnny Walker* show on several occasions, has presented papers at various conferences, seminars and journals, as well as having contributed to numerous international and national TV programmes (including *Heaven and Earth*, *Horizon*, *Everyman*, *This Morning* and *Open House*) on the subject of religion and paranormal phenomena.

Emma's main interests lie in the field of anthropology of religion and the psychology behind why people believe in the things they do. She is intrigued by visions and experiences and has a vast and unparalled database of first hand contemporary testimonies. She has researched numerous experiences including stigmata, alien encounters, simulacrums, visions of angels, Jesus and alleged miracles across the world. Emma moved into the area of religious broadcasting straight after her degree and still works in the media, assisting with the Sunday morning show for BBC Hereford and Worcester.

She continues to write and research in between working for more prime time television slots and films, with recent credits including ITV's *Star Lives*, *Soap Star Lives*, Channel 4's *Perfect Match* and two award-winning short film commissioned by Carlton Television.

Any letters will be forwarded to the author and can be sent care of John Blake Publishing, enclosing a self-addressed, stamped envelope if a reply is needed.

Media enquiries to Ailsa Macalister ailsa@colmacPR.co.uk Tel: 020 8671 6615/07711 675 608.

'The important thing is not to stop questioning'
ALBERT EINSTEIN